What Is Psychoanalysis?

WHAT IS
PSYCHOANALYSIS?

by

Ernest Jones, M. D.

New, revised and enlarged edition.

GREENWOOD PRESS, PUBLISHERS
WESTPORT, CONNECTICUT

Library of Congress Cataloging in Publication Data

Jones, Ernest, 1879–1958.
   What is psychoanalysis?

   Published in 1929 under title: Psycho-analysis.
   Bibliography: p.
   1. Psychoanalysis.   I. Title. [DNLM:
1. Psychoanalysis.   WM 460 J76ps 1948a]
BF173.J615 1973   150'.19'5   72-11478
ISBN 0-8371-6670-5

Originally published in 1948 by International Universities
Press, New York

Reprinted with the permission of International Universities
Press

Reprinted by Greenwood Press, Inc.

First Greenwood reprinting 1973
Second Greenwood reprinting 1977

Library of Congress catalog card number 72-11478

ISBN 0-8371-6670-5

Printed in the United States of America

CONTENTS

INTRODUCTION

CHAPTER I

WHAT IS PSYCHOANALYSIS?

POPULAR ideas about psychoanalysis seem to oscillate between two extremes. According to some, it is nothing but the translation into high-sounding jargon of platitudes that are well known to every writer about human nature, and, indeed, to every man of the world. According to others, on the contrary, it consists of a number of statements and conclusions that would be in the highest degree repellent were it not that the fantastic improbability of them prevents their being taken seriously. The truth, as so often, lies between the two.

While every endeavor will be made here to link the new discoveries of psychoanalysis to other, more familiar, knowledge, one cannot conceal the fact that they present many features of uniqueness. Psychoanalysis attempts to answer questions that had previously not been even raised, questions the very existence of which is often denied. It deals almost entirely with a field of knowledge, the unconscious mind, the existence of which is both unknown and denied. Much of its material, taken from neurotic patients, is concerned with a hinterland of semi-responsibility for which no place has been allotted in the scheme of society. Worse than all, the truths it announces as important discoveries are unwelcome, wounding, or repugnant, so that one cannot be surprised when they meet with general repudiation. Nevertheless, as the appearance of this volume witnesses, there is a certain uneasy demand for information about this extraordinary subject, a suspicion that there are unexplored depths in human nature, a half-recognition of echoes and reverberations aroused by the statements of psychoanalysts. Can there be, after all, an intuition that perhaps there may be something true and useful to be gleaned from this new science, that in time we may learn to tolerate and even profit from what it may have to say?

We shall meet with many paradoxes in this study, and so may as well begin with the first. The word "psychoanalysis" is used to denote three things, and the question is naturally asked how this can be so when the three things are so different in nature. "Psychoanalysis" means a special method of medical treatment devised by Professor Freud of Vienna for the cure of a certain class of nervous disorders; this restricted sense was the one in which it was first used. It also means a special technique for investigating the deeper layers of the mind. Lastly, it is used to describe the province of knowledge which has been won through the exercise of this method, and in this sense is practically synonymous with "the science of the unconscious". This third use of the word is, perhaps, intelligible as an obvious extension, but to understand how a method of investigation can be at the same time a method of treatment needs a knowledge of some of the most recondite problems in mental functioning. One would think that three meanings are quite enough for one technical term, but the reader should be warned that it is frequently, and quite illegitimately, used in several other senses, and this is by no means the least of the reasons for the confusion and difficulty in apprehending what psychoanalysis really is. The laity, and even some physicians, speak of psychoanalysis when they are referring to any form of psychotherapy (mental treatment of nervous disorders), irrespective of whether the technical method devised by Freud is employed or not. This happens still more often when a modicum of Freud's method and conclusions, often only imperfectly comprehended, is adopted but mixed with a leaven of other incompatibles. Then again, as one sees from publishers' advertisements and other sources of information, the term is commonly used to designate any psychological methods or conclusions that can be called at all modern, that belong, for instance, to the period since the first World War. It gets applied in these ways to matters that have either only a remote connection or none at all with psychoanalysis proper.

The question that gives the title to the present chapter will be answered, however sketchily, in the course of the whole book, and particularly in the second section. But before going into details it will be well to become clear about one of the most peculiar and outstanding features of the whole subject. That

the mind contains elements not accessible to consciousness had long been suspected and had been partly
established before Freud's time, but it was he who first
clearly recognized that they were in a state of dis-
harmony with the rest of the mind. In the course of
his investigations, by his technique which exposed its
most deeply buried constituents, he found that the
mind could in many respects be likened to a series of
water-tight compartments. Communication between
the different compartments is *actively* prevented by the
operation of perfectly definite factors, into the nature
of which he also inquired. His endeavors to open up
the deeper parts of the mind were thwarted by the
subject in ways that gave him the lively impression of
an opposing force, and so he did not hesitate to describe the state of affairs in dynamic terms. He spoke
of mental forces that were opposed to the subject's
becoming aware of certain parts of his mind, and he
called them *resistances*. He then made the brilliant
guess, an hypothesis that was soon amply confirmed,
that the forces he experienced as thwarting resistances
in his work of exploration were the same as those
that had originally prevented the person from knowing that part of his mind; in the latter form they are
called *repressions*. Now, we are all familiar with the
fact that there are various ideas, feelings, and wishes
within us the existence of which we would fain not
recognize and, in fact, often succeed in denying. We
simply would rather not know about them, and we
invent all sorts of reasons, some good and some bad,
why it would be better not to know about them and

wiser to "forget" them, to "put them out of our mind". This is a point where Freud's discoveries link on to common observation, but at the same time it cannot be stated too emphatically that the part of the mind he is referring to here has only a remote connection with the mental processes we consciously dislike within ourselves. Both the "resistances" in question and the part of the mind they are opposed to are entirely unknown to the subject's consciousness, and it is for this reason that Freud uses the term "unconscious" (German, *das Unbewusste*; literally, "the unapprehended"). How unconscious the unconscious is, only direct personal experience of it can enable one to appreciate, and one knows that this is not really conveyed by merely saying, however emphatically, that the person has absolutely not an inkling of the very existence of what is called the true unconscious. Further, the completeness of his ignorance is only equalled by the strength of the resistance that maintains this ignorance. This, perhaps, can be indicated by the statement that, even in favorable circumstances and with the use of the most refined technique, it often takes years of daily work to get a person to realize what mental processes are at work in the depths of his mind. The intensity of the inner resistance against full self-knowledge is one of the most important of Freud's discoveries.

Man, with all his seeking out of new things, has always displayed opposition to new ideas, opposition which has often enough been savage in its fierceness. Nor has he ever appeared to learn anything from this fact, familiar though it is. Attempts to understand it have hardly gone beyond such vague phrases as "innate conservatism". This general observation is not made here merely because the reception of psychoanalysis affords one more example of its truth: there is a much more interesting connection between the two than that. It is the merit of psychoanalysis, stimulated no doubt by its own experiences, to have offered an explanation of this fateful conservatism of mankind. Its explanation is that the general opposition to alien ideas, including those concerned with the outer world, is mainly a radiation of the inner opposition, or "resistance", against self-knowledge.

If we reflect on the well-known historical examples of this conservatism, such as that shown against astronomy in the sixteenth century, physiology in the seventeenth, chemistry in the eighteenth, and biology in the nineteenth, we cannot fail to be struck by certain stereotyped features it presents. The most prominent manifestations of it are anger and hostility, which naturally tend to express themselves in acts of persecution against the offender; the anger characteristically assumes the form of righteous indignation, and the new idea is often denounced as wicked and immoral. But it is not hard to detect behind this attitude, as perhaps behind all such attitudes in individual life, a note of unmistakable alarm. Something precious is felt to be threatened, and the hostile demonstrations are simply a reaction of defense against an imagined attack.

The complaints made against the new knowledge are almost monotonous in their sameness. It will destroy or impair some precious possession; it is degrading, materialistic, or even atheistic. It will reduce man from his high level, injure his good opinion of himself, or take away from him something that he holds most dear. This something is nearly always of an aesthetic, spiritual, ethical, or religious nature, something that man treasures as his highest good. Let us consider a simple example—Keats' fear that the knowledge gained about the rainbow through spectrum analysis would impair or take away his aesthetic enjoyment of the phenomenon. We can learn from such an example that such fears always prove in time to be illusory. Keats felt that his enjoyment of the rainbow was inherently dependent on a sense of mystery, and he imagined that the light of knowledge would dispel this, thus removing the necessary condition for his enjoyment. There are two answers to this attitude. In the first place, no scientific man could feel that any gain in knowledge weakens his sense of wonder at the universe. On the contrary: to know more can only teach one how little is known and how much is, perhaps, unknowable. Humility at the unknown increases as the illusions born of ignorance are dispelled. Yet man clings to both the illusions and the ignorance. In the second place, psychoanalysis can throw light on the nature of the illusory fear that mystery and ignorance are necessary in order to retain what may broadly be called the sense of spiritual value.

There is reason to hope that the dread of science is slowly diminishing. There would seem to be a little more capacity to tolerate this dread than in bygone ages. Certainly the only noticeable progress man has made in the past five or ten thousand years is closely associated with an increase in this tolerance and the confidence it begets. After all, experience produces its effect sooner or later, and some day man will realize that he gains instead of loses by exchanging humility and confidence for arrogance and fear. Psychoanalysis puts this matter once more to a severe test. But more than this, it advances the high claim of enabling man to deal finally with the dark fears that have hitherto so enslaved him.

We can here only indicate the approach to this great problem. It is not hard to see that it is bound up with the question of free will, for this is closely associated with our spiritual sense of the infinite and absolute. In our early history the conception of causality evidently had an extremely restricted scope. The most important happenings in life were believed to be arbitrary volitional intrusions into whatever slight order there might appear to be in the universe. For ages this volitional power has been divided in varying degree between human and supernatural beings, and, as the latter could frequently be induced to exercise their powers in accord with the wishes of the former, man could believe that he exerted through his will-power alone a very considerable influence over the happenings that most nearly concerned his welfare. The growth of civilization is commensurate with man's gradual renunciation of this illusory power. Experience slowly teaches him that to recognize the existence of natural law gives him more real power in exchange for what he renounces, but each time it costs him a painful effort. The inexorable demand of science is that no event shall be regarded as isolated, only as a link in the chain of inevitable sequence. This holds good for the processes of the human mind as strictly as for any other, and psychoanalysis has committed the offence of applying to the study of the mind this general scientific attitude. It has not helped matters to point out at the same time that the personal sense of free will and free choice is a very real thing and that there is an important meaning in the apparently paradoxical phrase of some persons being mentally freer than others. The wound remains, and people refuse to believe that the whole edifice of personal responsibility, social ethics, individual taste and judgment is not being violently threatened. Nevertheless, in time it will be seen that this attempt to apprehend order in apparent chaos, to show that the wildest flights of the fancy and the deepest yearnings of the soul are all part of the harmony of the universe, can only have the same result as previous advances in science. It can only heighten man's real power, and in this instance where he is most in need of it, over himself.

CHAPTER II

THE HISTORY OF PSYCHOANALYSIS

THE GERM of psychoanalysis is to be found in a curious observation made nearly fifty years ago by a Viennese physician, Dr. Breuer. He noticed that various hysterical symptoms from which a patient of his suffered disappeared when he got her to recall in a waking state a particular forgotten memory that she had recovered during hypnosis. The memory in question was the first appearance of the individual symptom. It was thus shown that the existence of the symptom depended on an amnesia (loss of memory), on something in its history having been forgotten, and that the symptom could be removed by destroying this essential condition.

This observation, of limited medical interest, may seem to be almost trivial, but it fertilized the mind of a genius to produce a lifetime of pioneering work in psychology, the general significance of which we are now beginning to perceive. Freud, a younger colleague of Breuer's, made use of the observation when the exigencies of life compelled him to give up anatomical research for neurological practice. He found himself faced with the bewildering congeries of hysterical

symptoms that come today and go tomorrow, that shift
in the most rambling fashion from one part of the body
to another, and he set himself the task of understanding them. At that time the problem itself did not
exist, for it had not occurred to anyone that such
phenomena could have a psychological meaning; they
were supposed either to be dependent on an underlying disease of the brain or to be created in the most
arbitrary manner by the disordered imagination of the
patient, i. e., to be a good example of the exercise of
free will. The field, therefore, was virginal, and it
looked unpromising enough.

One often hears the idea expressed that Freud
began his work with a preconceived theory which he
forced on the observations he collected. Nothing could
be further from the actual truth. Nothing could be
more unlike a philosophical theory than the development of the theory of psychoanalysis, which has always
consisted of direct inference from verifiable observations. It has grown piece by piece, errors and imperfect conclusions have been retracted, the first glimpses
replaced by more comprehensive vision, just exactly
as experience deepened and the field of observation
widened. Few people could have been more astonished
than Freud himself at many of his findings, which
were quite unexpected. All that he had at the outset
of his scientific career, besides his native gifts and
restless curiosity, were Breuer's observation alluded
to above and an unshakeable conviction that mental
phenomena, even the most trivial and fugitive, must
have as precise antecedents as physical ones. To ex-

plain them by such phrases as "chance", "coinci-
dence", "habit", "laziness", and the like was completely unsatisfying to him, for his belief in determinism was thorough-going. He was born for research,
and both his lot and his inclination took him to the
field of psychology.

Freud soon confirmed Breuer's observation that
both the occurrence of hysterical symptoms and the
form they assumed depended on events in the patient's
past life. The memory of these events, which could
often be recovered during hypnosis, was commonly
forgotten and yet it was not dead; on the contrary, it
was responsible for current happenings and suffering.
Inaccessible memories, therefore, were not always
merely latent, like forgotten names that may be re-
suscitated through chance associations, but could also
be active. Freud thus developed the conception of a
dynamic unconscious, one previously imagined by
philosophers like Schopenhauer and von Hartmann,
but never before actually explored. More will be said
in the succeeding chapter about this conception, which
is fundamental in psychoanalysis.

Within a few years of beginning this work, Freud
was faced with a difficulty which resulted in what was,
perhaps, his greatest act of creative inventiveness. The
difficulty consisted in his coming across patients whom
neither he nor more experienced experts could hypno-
tize; he therefore had to give up the hope of carrying
out his therapeutic investigation with such patients
or else alter his methods. He began by urging the
patient to concentrate and recollect in a waking state

and found that the genesis of the particular symptom could generally be traced in this way, so he at once abandoned the further use of hypnotism. Experience then showed him that the forgotten memories connected with the genesis of the various symptoms in a given case were closely interconnected, so that it was a question of laying bare this network rather than vainly attempting to isolate and unravel each individual symptom in turn. It was at this point that he most boldly tested his faith in determinism and in the truth of his previous conclusions about the unconscious. Acting on the assumption that something must be directing a train of thought, even when it appeared to be freely wandering, and that this something could only be the influence of unconscious thoughts, he asked his patients to refrain from concentrating on any particular idea and from consciously guiding their thoughts; they had merely to relate to him the direction in which their thoughts went "of their own accord". This was the "free association method", the essential basis of all analytic technique. It yields the material for any psychoanalysis, though one should not, of course, confound it with the psychoanalysis itself, as some physicians appear to.

Already in the days of hypnotism Freud had observed that he had to exert a certain pressure on the patients, in the form of constant urging, before they could reproduce the requisite memories, and this feature was still more evident when he replaced the earlier method (called Breuer's cathartic method) by his free association method. He felt that the exertion he was aware of putting forth must be acting against some opposing force in the patient's mind, and he termed this opposition their resistance. As was mentioned above, the next step in the theory was to infer that this resistance was the very force that had originally kept the memory concerned from the patient's consciousness, had, as he termed it, "repressed" the memory. His dynamic conception of the unconscious thus expanded. Not only were repressed mental processes capable of producing active effects in spite of their being unconscious—i. e., in spite of the patient's being unaware of them—but another part of the mind was in active conflict with them, also without the patient's knowing anything about the state of affairs. This conclusion fitted in very well with another discovery which enabled him to say something about the nature of the conflict. For he found that the repressed memories which were producing these morbid effects were always of a special kind: they were incompatible with the moral, social, or aesthetic standards of the main personality and were therefore unwelcome discoveries to the patient. This he took to be the explanation of why they had been "repressed".

Before long it became clear to Freud that the unconscious conflicts with which he had to deal in his treatment of neurotic patients were of such a kind that they could not possibly be peculiar to them: all that was peculiar to them was the particular way in which they had automatically tried to cope with the conflicts, a way that entailed the production of neurotic symptoms. The conflicts themselves were common to all humanity, and so Freud was insensibly led on to consider matters of general psychological interest. The knowledge he had gained about the workings of the unconscious proved to be a key to the understanding of many other problems besides the original ones he had set out to solve in connection with the neuroses. Incidentally, it also showed that neurotics were not a distinct class incomparable with the rest of humanity, as had previously been supposed, and, further, that neuroses were not "diseases" in the accepted sense. Neuroses were seen to be merely one of the many different ways in which people react to psychological and social difficulties that everyone has to meet. To say that it is illegitimate to transfer to the normal conclusions reached in the study of the abnormal is simply to display an ignorance of what neuroses really mean.

A few of the fields in normal psychology to which Freud extended his investigations may be mentioned at this point, though they will be considered at greater length later on. In the material of free association supplied by patients, dreams played such a part that Freud was led to inquire into a subject which had at that time been greatly neglected by psychologists and physicians. For this purpose he mainly used, at least in his exposition, his own dreams, so as to avoid the criticism we have just mentioned about "abnormal material". He was able to solve a number of age-old problems, and his study of dreams ranks as one of his most important contributions, not only because of the practical value that the analysis of dreams has for the exploration of the deeper layers of the mind (Freud himself called it the royal road to the unconscious), but especially because it was one of the most comprehensive and finished of all his works. The resemblance between many dream mechanisms and those observable in the production of wit aroused his interest in this latter subject, and he devoted a penetrating study to the elucidation of the unconscious processes underlying wit and applied problems of aesthetics (humor, the comic, the uncanny, and so forth).

In his investigation of the neuroses Freud found that sexual factors played both an invariable and an essential part in the pathogenic conflict, and the characteristic thoroughness with which he persisted in tracing back the entire chain of events as far as he could, to the beginnings if possible, resulted in his learning much that was new about the early stages in the development of this instinct. The next book he wrote, after those on dreams and wit, dealt with this subject. Among the repressed impulses that constituted one-half of the unconscious conflict sexual ones are predominant as, indeed, is not surprising, and this particular form of conflict was soon perceived to be by far the commonest and most important. A much larger proportion of the sexual instinct leads an underground life than is generally imagined, and the energy derived from it has a peculiar capacity for being transferred to other interests, the result being that an unexpected amount of our conscious activities are in part dependent on repressed sexual impulses. It is, as might be expected, about these conclusions that the greater part of the opposition to psychoanalysis centres.

Freud's method of work being essentially a genetic one, it is not surprising that the chief part of it is ultimately concerned with problems of child development, and here also he has reached a number of novel conclusions, particularly over the much debated question of the child's sexual life. Resemblances between the mental processes characteristic of childhood and of neurotics on the one hand, and of uncivilized adults on the other gave Freud the occasion to make a series of contributions to the nature of myth and superstition and to the social and religious institutions of savages, and these have thrown a flood of light on obscure problems concerned with the past history of the race. Altogether he draws a close parallel between the processes of development in the individual and those in the race.

This broad outline of some of the fields in which Freud has worked convey no idea at all of the enormous mass of detailed contributions he has made to specific problems. The only purpose in sketching it is to give some notion of the way in which psychoanalysis first began and the historical reasons for its having followed the path of development it has, notably in regard to the central part played by the study of neurotic patients. It is this study that forms the permanent basis of psychoanalysis, for experience with the so-called normal has shown that it is extra-ordinarily difficult to proceed far in the exploration of the unconscious except by the aid of phenomena which, when exaggerated, are called neurotic.

About the external development of the science of
psychoanalysis little need be said here. For more than
ten years Freud worked quite alone, his studies finding neither sympathy nor acceptance. Other physicians
then adopted his methods and confirmed and extended
his findings; the present writer, for instance, has been
working on these lines for over forty years. In 1910
an International Association of Psychoanalysis was
founded with constituent branches in various countries, the British branch being formed in 1913; by
now, there are branch societies in many countries. A
large number of periodicals are devoted to the subject,
and the literature on it, much of which is of very un-
equal value, is immense. There are numerous Insti-
tutes of Psychoanalysis, with clinics attached, where
systematic courses of instruction are given in the practice and technique of the methods and in the general
theory of the findings. Two former adherents of Freud
—Adler and Jung—after a short period of co-operation abjured his methods and conclusions and founded
independent systems of psychology, which largely con-
sist in denials of Freud's.

CONTENT OF PSYCHOANALYSIS

CHAPTER I

THE UNCONSCIOUS

To ASSUME the existence of mental processes of which we are totally unaware, i. e., an unconscious mind, is to take a serious step in thought which has far-reaching consequences, and it is little wonder that those who shrink from it seek for support in a variety of rationalistic and philosophical arguments. The main one consists in the dictum that since the word "mental" signifies by definition "conscious", there cannot be anything mental that is not conscious; if non-conscious processes have been discovered by psychoanalysis, they must be physical in nature. This view clearly dates from a time before the question was raised, and, indeed, is little more than an assertion that has always been taken for granted. If the statement is seriously made that these unconscious processes are, in reality, physical and not mental, one may demand some evidence for it, which has never been forthcoming. It need hardly be said that no physiological studies give us the slightest information about these particular unconscious processes, whereas, on the other hand, they can be readily described in the customary mental terms, as ideas, wishes, and so forth. Incidentally, investigations by means of hypnotism, apart altogether from psychoanalysis, have long afforded plain indications of their mental nature. After all, to describe the unconscious as mental is merely a special application of a procedure we use every day in our dealings with other human beings. We have no immediate knowledge of anyone's mentality other than our own, but we unhesitatingly infer its existence through identification of ourselves with other people. When, therefore, we have similarly good grounds to infer the presence of mental activity in ourselves without being directly aware of it, and especially when, as often happens, the activity in question resembles conscious mentation in all respects except in the sole one of not being conscious, it is surely simplest to call it also mental. We certainly should not hesitate to do so were it not that there are inner resistances, connected with the content of the unconscious, which struggle against the recognition of this part of the mind. Be all that as it may, however, psychoanalysis would find it quite impossible to set forth its findings and conclusions except in terms of an unconscious mind, for its main work consists in the unravelling of unconscious processes, which can be described only in mental language and in converting them into conscious processes.

As his insight and knowledge concerning these deeper layers of the mind became more comprehensive, Freud gradually formulated a theory of the structure of the mind as a whole. We cannot here trace the detailed steps in the development of the theory, and shall content ourselves with depicting three important aspects of it at the present day. In the first place, Freud regards the mind somewhat as an apparatus which can be set in motion in two different ways, from without and from within. Stimuli impinging on the mind from without, through excitation of the sense organs, start activity from one direction, while stimuli from within, such as hunger or any other instinctive agency, start it from another; in many cases, such as when a hungry man sees a tempting morsel, both kinds of stimulation occur together. Freud thinks that all of these mental acts are to begin with unconscious, but that some pass through into consciousness instantaneously, while others are prevented from doing so. That the instinctive stimuli, arising from within the organism, proceed from or through an unconscious region is not hard to understand, but many instances from daily life can show us how the same may be true also with the outer stimuli: thus it often happens that we can prove to ourselves that something in us must have heard a given sound, say, the striking of a clock, when we have no memory of having consciously heard it at the time.

Judging mental processes in their relation to consciousness, Freud finds it necessary to postulate three groups, which, if one wishes to form a picture in space, may be regarded as occupying three areas of the mind. First there is ordinary consciousness, comprising all the thoughts we are aware of at a given moment. Then there is what is called the preconscious, a sort of antechamber to consciousness. All preconscious thoughts can become conscious in appropriate circumstances, either through an effort of will in' recollection or through their being stimulated by an associated idea. Though this is so, one can, nevertheless, distinguish two sub-groups of preconscious thoughts, those of which one can become aware without much difficulty, readily accessible memories and the like, and those about whose becoming conscious there is an appreciable or even a considerable difficulty. Experience shows that the latter group have special associative connections with unconscious material, and this no doubt accounts for the difficulty in question. Finally, there is the true unconscious, consisting of thoughts which are quite incapable of becoming conscious unless a special manipulative activity is brought about by an analytic procedure.

There would appear to be a selective agency at work on which depends the admission of a given thought from one of these mental compartments to another, and Freud, using an analogy with a political institution familiar to us all during wars, calls this agency a "censorship". The main censorship is certainly that interposed between the unconscious and the preconscious, but there is also a weaker one between the preconscious and consciousness itself. The agency effecting this censorship is identical with the "repression" mentioned earlier, i. e., the keeping of certain thoughts out of consciousness, and again with the "resistance" manifested against any endeavor to make such thoughts conscious, to make a person aware of them.

Leaving now this matter of consciousness and unconsciousness, we have next to consider the mind from another point of view, from what may be called a dynamic point of view instead of a topographical one. It will not be quite easy to combine the two pictures thus obtained, for the classification is in some respects a crossed one. The very depths of the mind, roughly corresponding with the popular idea of the unconscious and certainly possessing neither the attributes of consciousness nor any sense of personality, comprise a number of primordial impulses and instinctive urges that are constantly welling up, as it were, and pressing forward to find some relief or satisfaction. Because of its impersonal nature, indicated, by the way, by such expressions as "it seems to me", "it feels to me to be", which are commoner in other languages than English, Freud refers to this region of the mind as the "it", for which we generally use the Latin word *id*. The id is the fount of mental energy derived from the instincts. It is the quite undifferentiated basis of the whole mind.

In the early days of development a portion of this id becomes marked off from the rest through contact with the outer world. This portion, whose main function is to establish relations between the individual organism and the outer world, including the human environment, Freud terms the *ego*. It comprises, of course, the self in ordinary language, that which gives us the sense of personality. By no means all the ego belongs to consciousness, which is contrary to expectation; very important parts of it are unconscious in the full sense of the word, as defined above

—i. e., quite inaccessible to consciousness. There is early established a certain critical attitude on the part of the ego towards the rest of the id, which we may now call the id, pure and simple. It accepts part of the demands for gratification made by the id impulses, but it condemns and rejects others. This latter process is the same as what we have learned to call repression, so that this word refers not only to the keeping apart from consciousness, but also to the keeping apart from the ego. The repressed impulses thus form another special section of the primitive id; they are, of course, impersonal. The state of affairs might therefore be rendered by some such phrases as these: "I (myself, the ego) wish to do this and this; some other thing in me, not myself, wants to do that and that," provided it is remembered that the conscious self is unaware of the second wish.

One last complication in this connection remains to be noted. Just as a part of the id becomes split off as the repressed id, so does a part of the ego become in the course of development differentiated from the rest; it is termed the *superego*. The function of the superego, which is in closer contact with the id than is the ego, is to watch over the relations between the two, to act, as it were, as a guard that warns the ego of the danger of accepting any repressed impulses emanating from the id. This function is familiar to us under the name of censorship, but it should be noted that, strictly speaking, it is the ego itself that performs the act of repression, not the superego; it commonly does so, however, at the dictation of the latter. It is a matter of special interest that the superego comes into existence in response to the influence of the parents in the first years of life; it is far from being a direct copy of their teaching, but it owes most of its strength to the emotional tie between child and parent.

To sum up, we see that there are four instances in the mind: first, the primitive id, from which a part becomes differentiated as the ego; the part of the id that is incompatible with the standards of the ego constitutes the repressed portion, whereas, on the other hand, a part of the ego becomes differentiated into a separate superego. All this may sound a little reminiscent of an ancient mythology, where distinct deities were endowed with particular functions, but the effect of personification is solely due to the necessity for a condensed description. Actually Freud considers that the various attitudes and functions mentioned are brought about just as automatically as are those pertaining to the body itself, and he expressly maintains that the idea of personality is confined to the ego alone. This is one reason among others, incidentally, why a person to whom the presence of these unconscious processes is demonstrated finds at first a difficulty in recognizing that they are actually part of himself.

It will readily be understood that repressed impulses are what would ordinarily be called immoral. Strictly speaking, they would be called immoral if they were exposed to a moral judgment; actually they are non-moral, for no feeling of right or wrong attaches to them. They are either sexual or hostile (cruel, aggressive) in nature, but most of the hostility is engendered as a result of sexual impulses being thwarted, so that one may say that repressed impulses are predominantly sexual. On the other side, the superego is the most moral part of the whole organism, and it is much more "moral" than the moral conscience we are familiar with. In one sense it may, therefore, be said that, according to psychoanalysis, man proves to be both more immoral and more moral than he knew.

If the superego constituted in early childhood fails to develop freely, fateful consequences may follow. It is well known that children are apt at a certain age to be over-moral, that is, to regard slight lapses from the standards they have recently acquired as being heinous sins with tragic significance; much of the unhappiness of childhood comes from this. If the childish attitude just indicated persists, or if it is directed against remote derivatives of the forbidden impulses, then all sorts of quite innocent acts, even those such as walking, eating, and so on, may become forbidden in adult years. To consciousness this forbiddenness appears simply as incapacity, which constitutes one form of nervous disorder. An important step in the treatment of nervous troubles is often the lightening of this burden of irrational guilt.

Preconscious processes usually differ from conscious ones in no respects except that the attribute of consciousness is missing. Those of the unconscious proper, on the other hand, possess a number of characteristics that quite mark them off from conscious ones, and some of these are in striking contradistinction to those of conscious processes. Some have already been hinted at: such are their close relation to the instincts and to infantile life, their conative (wish) nature, and the prominent part displayed in them by sexuality. There are many others which cannot be described here. As examples, however, may be mentioned the total absence in the unconscious of the ideas of time and of negation; the unconscious is quite timeless, and the word "no" has no significance for it. The ideas present are non-verbal representations of objects or acts, words being confined to conscious or preconscious processes. The energy belonging to these ideas, or rather to the impulses they represent, is very mobile, and can be shifted from one to another in a way that is quite foreign to conscious mental life. The unconscious is entirely regulated according to the pleasure-pain principle, which is the sole criterion in its functioning. In the course of development this evolves into the reality-principle, in which other considerations than simple pleasure or pain matter, but this operates only in the higher layers of the mind. One must lay stress, therefore, on the fact that unconscious processes have many peculiarities of their own which make them very different from conscious ones.

CHAPTER II

REPRESSION AND CONFLICT

THE GENERAL SIGNIFICANCE of repression and of conflict within the mind has already been indicated, and we have here mainly to consider some of their effects. The aim of repression—if such a teleological expression, unavoidable in the interests of brevity, be permitted—is nothing less than the obliterating of the offending repressed impulse against which it is directed. It does at times even appear to succeed in inhibiting the impulse almost entirely, but this must be very rare, and probably always temporary. In the vast majority of cases it succeeds only partly, and the repressed impulse manages to find some sort of expression. A great part of psychoanalysis is taken up with tracing the fate of these buried impulses and the tortuous manifestations they produce on their path towards gratification.

An outstanding characteristic of the unconscious is the extent to which the energy of the impulses composing it can be displaced along paths of association. The result is that one idea can serve to carry the significance of another "associated" one. The function of the first one, or rather the impulse it represents, can

34

thus be discharged through the second one. If there is a complicated chain of associations functioning in this way through displacement and other mechanisms, the unravelling of it produces on the conscious mind a lively impression of something alien and far-fetched. This impression, often imputed to the psychoanalytic procedure, is more properly to be ascribed to the nature of unconscious functioning, which, as has already been pointed out, differs in this respect as in so many others from that of consciousness. An allied mechanism may also be mentioned in this connection, that of condensation. By this is meant the propensity of unconscious processes to fuse together on a very slight pretext, and in this way to reinforce one another. The unconscious is interested only in resemblances; it ignores distinctions in an astonishing measure, and does not discriminate in the way the conscious mind does. The consequence is that any manifestation of the unconscious is nearly always what is called "over-determined", that is to say, it is the resultant of many determining factors.

There are four chief issues to the conflict between the ego and the repressed, and we shall now proceed to describe them. In one of them, the second, the resulting manifestation is composed altogether of material derived from the ego impulses; in the other three it is compounded of material derived from both the ego and the repressed impulses, so that they are in the nature of compromises. In one of them, the first, there is a qualitative change in the nature of the energy of the impulse, in the succeeding two this is not so, while the fourth is in this respect midway between the other two groups.

1. *Sublimation.* By this is meant a change in a sexual impulse whereby it becomes "desexualized", that is, it loses the peculiar exciting quality characteristic of sexuality, and it is deflected towards a nonsexual goal. It is not common for this to happen with an adult, fully developed sexual impulse; it happens much more frequently with the component parts of the sexual instinct, which we shall discuss in a future chapter. The process is, of course, like all those here described, a quite unconscious one. It is important to note that the conscious result of the process is not a substitute of something else for the sexual interest, as is commonly thought, but the same thing in another form. Thus, when sport or dancing is said to be healthy and wholesome for the young, by which is really meant that it turns their attention away from sexual preoccupations, it owes much of its capacity for this to the fact that it is in large part a transformation of various sexual impulses the energy of which flows into the other activity. The numerous outlets for maternal impulses are, perhaps, the most familiar examples of sublimation. Sublimations are of varying degrees of stability. In certain circumstances they tend to "regress" towards their original significance, when the person loses interest in the previous activity and is on the way to developing a neurosis. This is the real explanation of most cases of "nervous breakdown from over-work".

2. *Reaction-formation.* In contradistinction to

sublimations, where the energy is not only derived from the repressed impulse but flows in the same direction as it, that of reaction-formations is derived from the opposing ego forces and is aimed in exactly the opposite direction. They might, indeed, be described by the more static metaphor of barriers erected as dams against the repressed impulses. The contrast between them and sublimations may be illustrated by a couple of examples. The primitive tendency to self-display (of the person) may be sublimated into a taking of pleasure in self-prominence, either physically as in oratory or, more indirectly still, as in the many varieties of fame-seeking, or, on the other hand, it may lead to the reaction of modesty, shame, and the like. The primitive pleasure all children take in dirt may be sublimated into painting, sculpture work, or cooking, or it may lead to the reaction of cleanliness, tidiness (dirt is matter in the wrong place!), and similar traits. On the policy of "mak siccar" it is very common for reaction-formations to overstep the mark and to become excessive. We have all known, for instance, the house-wife whose intolerance for dust makes life a burden for those around her. It is also common for extremes to meet in this connection: an unduly strong reaction-formation points to the presence of an unduly strong impulse behind it, and sometimes the positive and the negative are shown on different occasions in the same person, as when someone is absurdly mean in some respect and immoderately extravagant in another.

3. *Neurosis.* This outcome of unconscious conflict

will form the subject of Chapter VI of the present section, so that a word or two about it will suffice here. Every neurotic disorder is a compromise between the repressing forces and the repressed impulses, both of which come to expression in the neurotic manifestations. In this case the chief repressed impulses are invariably sexual and the sexual quality is not altered as it is with sublimation. Both sets of forces constituting the conflict undergo an extensive distortion before they are manifested in the form of neurotic suffering; the symptoms, therefore, have to be analyzed before their meaning is disclosed.

4. *Character formation.* On the way in which the various unconscious conflicts are dealt with in early life the greater part of the later character will depend. A large number of character traits, such as determination, ambitiousness, timidity, tenacity, and so on, have been traced to particular reactions in regard to these conflicts. It sometimes happens that the transformation into character traits has been imperfect, the traits in question still betraying evidence of unconscious characteristics (in addition to that of their unconscious origin, which is, of course, always present). The term "neurotic character" is applied in such cases, for the traits are manifestations intermediate between normal character traits and neurotic symptoms. When a neurosis is, so to speak, built into the character in this way it is much harder to eradicate than in the more usual cases where it is foreign to the main personality and is felt to be an imposed affliction.

Symbolism. Something may be said about this

interesting subject here, although its precise relation to the themes of repression and conflict is still obscure. The subject is an important one in psychoanalytic work and has also been the occasion of much critical comment. Some of the latter arises from a pure confusion about the word "symbolism", for it is commonly used in very different senses. The various statements made by psychoanalysts about symbolism relate entirely to a special restricted sense of the word in which by *"symbol" is meant an idea in consciousness that represents and carries the significance of another, unconscious, idea.* A symbol in the psychoanalytic sense is a pure substitute for an unconscious idea and thus differs altogether from such processes as simile and metaphor, the ones with which we are ordinarily familiar. An enormous number of ideas, mostly of concrete objects or processes, may serve in a symbolic function, but the notion commonly imputed to analysts that such ideas are to be regarded as symbols wherever they occur is, of course, absurd. It is often a matter of considerable technical difficulty to decide when an idea possesses its literal intrinsic signification or is functioning symbolically. It has been estimated that the number of ideas in the unconscious that can be symbolized is at most a hundred, and that they are all concerned with ideas of the self and the immediate blood relations or of the phenomena of birth, love, and death. The alleged monotony of psychoanalytic interpretations of symbols is thus due ultimately to the extreme concentration of the most primitive interests of man as represented in the deepest layers of his mind. A couple of typical symbols may be mentioned illustratively. The ideas of king and queen, on the occasions when they function symbolically, always mean father and mother respectively, parting means death, and rescue, most characteristically out of water, means childbirth. There is a remarkable stereotypy in these meanings, though they are by no means invariable, and this again is a feature to which the critics have objected. The interpretation of symbols plays a considerable part in the analysis of dreams and neurotic symptoms.

CHAPTER III

SEXUALITY

THIS is certainly the theme on which the main opposition to psychoanalysis centres. Misunderstandings and misrepresentations about the tenets of psychoanalysis are correspondingly frequent here. In the first place it is often said that Freud extends the use of the word "sexual" so unjustifiably as to render misunderstanding inevitable. It is true that Freud applies the term "sexual" much more widely than is customary, but, strictly speaking, it is not so much the meaning of the word that he extends as the conceptions denoted by the word. It would simplify matters if one took it that when Freud uses the word "sexual",* he wishes to convey the same connotation as anyone else. The complication appears in two ways. For certain reasons Freud may come to the conclusion that the pleasure derived from a certain act, e. g., from nail-biting, is essentially sexual, a conclusion that is often startling. But he is not using the word in any esoteric sense; he

---

* At this point it is desirable to deprecate the confusion that arises from the common mistake of using the word "sex" where "sexual" is meant. A sex conflict, for instance, is a conflict over the subject of sex, i. e., the distinction between masculinity and femininity: a sexual conflict is any conflict over the subject of sexuality.

really means that the pleasure is sexual in the ordinary sense of the word. Then, again, he may maintain that another kind of pleasure, though not sexual in itself, is derived from sexual sources by a process of transformation. Thus the pleasure in dancing, one which is usually more or less (occasionally less than more) desexualized, is found to be derived from sexual ideas and wishes present in the unconscious and these are actually present there during the act of dancing.

The heavy social ban that is laid on various aspects of sexuality, and the extent to which ideas of morality are concentrated against all sorts of radiations from this central sin (the very word "immoral" is commonly used as an equivalent for "sexual"), is only an echo of the internal repression of sexual impulses, a consideration which will perhaps give some faint idea of how strong and deep the latter must be. The greater part of this internal repression is unconscious, so that we are referring to a quite different matter from ordinary conscious prejudice. It is, therefore, not surprising to learn that the part played in the unconscious by sexual impulses is very much more extensive than the part they play in consciousness. Nor is it surprising that any attempt to resist the ban on them by disclosing them is apt to evoke active opposition. This often takes the emotional form of absolute generalization, as when Freud is accused of being "sex-mad", of "reducing everything to sex", or of "pan-sexualism". Freud has certainly in his work dealt extensively with sexual problems among many others, but if only they had been chemical or physiological problems he could have specialized far more extensively without evoking such outbursts.

The part of his conclusions that has proved the most unacceptable undoubtedly relates to the sexuality of childhood. His experience directly contravenes the popular view that the sexual instinct first manifests itself during adolescence (or, in the case of girls, only after the ceremony of marriage, when it suddenly appears out of the blue), and that any signs of it during childhood are to be regarded as a diseased precocity. He maintains, on the contrary, that children conceal the sexual nature of their interests from themselves and still more from adults, while the latter reciprocate by ignoring them or else by punishing them as being simply "naughty"; only a general conspiracy of silence and blindness could manage to overlook facts that are patent for everyone to see, such facts as the bodily preoccupations and habits of children, their curiosities, loves, jealousies, and so on. He considers that the sexual instinct is active from the first day of life to the last, but that it manifests itself in a greater variety of ways, the nature of which is often unrecognized, than is generally supposed. For instance, it is quite misleading to confine our consideration of such matters to the sexual organs alone, for there is ample evidence that many other parts of the body, lips, breasts, and so forth, take an equally characteristic, if subordinate, share in the whole process, and that in certain circumstances (in the so-called perversions) these subordinate interests may attain the importance that usually attaches to more central ones.

According to psychoanalysis the sexual instinct is a complicated one. It is made up of various components that have to fuse into an entity, and often fail in doing so. It has to undergo a rather elaborate course of development during which various difficulties may arise, errors in development, arrest at certain stages ("fixations"), and so on. Most remarkable of all is the fact that this development has to be passed through twice over, a feature apparently peculiar to man. The two periods of life at which this happens are in early childhood, below the age of five, and in the years following puberty. In the interval (the "latency period") there is no progress in this development. The relationship between the two stages of development is highly interesting. Naturally they are not identical; the physical and mental differences between the child and the adult make this impossible. Nor is the development of the individual in general a simple repetition of the evolution of the race. But in both cases there is a considerable parallelism and the second development is very extensively determined by the nature of the first. The sexual development after puberty, for instance, assumes a multitude of forms, no two individuals being exactly alike in this respect as in any other, but the main lines on which it takes place, and often astonishing details, are already laid down in the first, childhood, phase. This is the reason why it is impossible either to understand or to remedy any errors in the second, puberty, phase (together

with their complicated consequences in neurotic dis--
orders) without taking into due account the features
in the first phase that determined those of the second
one. All memory of that first phase is usually obliterat-
ed during the great wave of repression that accompa-
nies this period of childhood; a part of it was, indeed,
not conscious even at the time and can be recovered
only by the psychoanalytic opening-up of the unconscious.

A very brief account of the first development will
now be given, first from the point of view of the
nature of the sexual activity itself and then from that
of its objects. The first stage of all is termed the oral
one, the activity consisting of the various forms of
sucking and swallowing; it can be subdivided into
two phases, sucking and biting respectively. To begin
with, the nutritional and oral-erotic impulses are in-
distinguishable from each other, the act being the
same with both, but it soon becomes evident that sucking has acquired some significance of its own quite
independent of hunger; every nurse knows how a
child's restlessness can be stilled by giving it a "comforter", and this need have nothing to do with any
desire for food. Later on the child replaces the nipple
and comforter by its thumb (often continued into
nail-biting and allied habits) and by any suitable and
interesting object. Even in adult life the lips continue
to function in this sense, for kissing is plainly nothing
but an attenuated form of sucking, and more complicated performances in which the mouth plays a part
are common enough. The second stage, called the anal-

sadistic one, is characterized by a curious combination of features. On the one hand, .there is the rough, noisy, obstreperous, and often cruel behavior which parents find so trying; on the other, there are various indications, less obtrusive than others, of interest, curiosity, secret games, and complicated mental attitudes relating to certain bodily needs. The third and final stage is the genital one, where these organs acquire the preponderating importance in this sphere which they then retain through life; on the mental side this stage is accompanied by development in the capacity for love and altruism.

From the point of view of the goal of these instinctive activities we may also perceive three stages. In the first, or auto-erotic one, there is, strictly speaking, no object; the child seeks for gratification in its own body, but there is hardly any sense of "I" and "it" in the proceeding. In the second stage, the narcissistic one, the ego has developed and is taken as the object of the instinct; one might say that the child loves itself, a capacity it never entirely gives up. The third stage is the critical one. Here the child seeks in the outer world for objects not only of its affection, but also of its conscious and unconscious sexual fantasies. It is inevitable that this should at first relate to those nearest to it, the members of its own family. Difficulties arise, however, when the fantasies (and often acts) indulged in with members of its own generation begin to be transferred to those of the older generation, principally the parents. This constitutes the famous *oedipus complex* in which there is a sexual attitude on the part of the child towards the parent of the opposite sex together with rivalry towards the one of its own; commonly enough there is also present an inverted oedipus complex where the reverse of this holds. This complex Freud regards as the central one in the whole unconscious; on the way in which the child deals with it depends more than on anything else its future character and temperament as well as any neurosis it may at any time develop. It is the most characteristic and important finding in all psycho-analysis, and against it is directed the whole strength of the individual's resistances as well as the external criticism of psychoanalysis. It is hardly an exaggeration to say that whatever manifold form this resistance may take, and whatever aspect of psychoanalysis is being criticized, it is the oedipus complex that is finally responsible. All other conclusions of psychoanalytic theory are grouped around this complex, and by the truth of this finding psychoanalysis stands or falls.

Nearly the whole of this chapter has been devoted to the theme of infantile sexuality. This is not only because it is the most novel and important of the psychoanalytic contributions to the present topic, but because it is this knowledge that furnishes the key to the understanding of adult problems. Every adult problem in the realm of sexuality, friction and difficulties in marriage, inadequacies in the conjugal relationships, the inner meaning of such social problems as the causes of prostitution or the emotions about birth-control, all jealousy, rivalry, and conflicts between the sexes, the origin of the various perverse practices and attitudes, and endless similar problems, all are capable of full explanation only in the light of our newly gained knowledge concerning the early stages in the development of this complicated instinct. In the psychoanalytic literature a flood of light has already been thrown on the significance and genesis of the mental attitudes indicated by the existence of such problems as those just mentioned, as well as very many others which cannot be even enumerated here.

CHAPTER IV

DREAMS

Freud's work on dreams was the first contact he established between psychoanalysis and general psychology. At the time (1900) dreams were universally regarded as unworthy of study by a serious scientific investigator, for it was believed that they were produced by irregular physical disturbances of the brain during sleep so that any attempt to read a psychological meaning into them savored of sooth-saying. It is true that the essence of Freud's theory of dreams has even yet not obtained any acceptance except at the hands of other analysts, but it has become recognized, thanks to his work, that the study of dreams is not only a serious, but a very important part of psychology, and further that it is of very great practical value in the treatment of nervous disorders where it is necessary to penetrate into the deeper layers of the mind.

The first point to grasp in the theory is the difference between the manifest content of the dream, i. e., the dream as recorded, and the latent content, i. e., the thoughts leading up to the dream which are ascertained by analyzing its details by the method of free association. In the construction of a dream nothing at all happens except the translation (technically called the dream work) of the latter set of mental processes into the other; for instance, no intellectual operation whatever is concerned. There is, however, much to be said about how this translation takes place and why it does, also about the origin of the latent thoughts in question.

The associations obtained by analysis comprise all manner of mental processes, wishes, fears, hopes, arguments, and so on, but Freud holds that the real kernel of them which is indispensable to the formation of any dream is a *wishfulfilment,* the imaginary gratification of a (mostly repressed) wish. By confining the analysis to the surface, and confounding the material thus obtained with the unconscious mechanism of the dream work proper, it is of course possible to maintain that dreams are of manifold origin, that they may proceed from fears alone, from attempts to solve current problems, and so on, and this mistake is commonly enough committed.

Freud maintains that the function of every dream is to *preserve sleep,* and that it does so (or attempts to do so) by converting into an imagined wishfulfilment any stimulus that threatens to disturb sleep, and in this way allaying the effect of the stimulus. The simplest type of dream, therefore, is that met with sometimes in young children, much more rarely among adults, in which a disturbing wish is simply gratified in the imagination; the thirsty man drinks freely and the hungry one enjoys a banquet. But matters are seldom so simple as this.

The disturbance may be of any nature, physical or mental, a pain in the stomach or the persistence of a worrying thought during sleep. In the majority of instances, in fact in all but exceptionally sound sleepers, the allaying of the disturbance is brought about in a more complicated way. The thought in question enters into association with a repressed wish, i. e., an unconscious and mostly infantile one, this repressed wish is imagined as gratified, and then the wishfulfilment undergoes an elaborate change before emerging into consciousness as the dream itself. The change is necessitated by the fact that what has to be represented belongs to the repressed part of the mind which is in itself incapable of reaching consciousness; before it can do so it has to pass the censorship which, as was pointed out in an earlier chapter, is interposed between the unconscious and consciousness. If the intensity of the repressed wish is too great the dream work is unable to perform this necessary task, the dream fails in its function, and the sleeper wakes. He has to wake so as to deal with the danger of the unconscious impulse that is on the point of emerging, and this can be done better in the waking state when the activity of the censoring agency is much greater; many thoughts, for instance, are admitted to consciousness during sleep (in a dream) that could not be in a waking state. Dreams of this sort are often accompanied by great fear or some other unpleasant emotion and they are naturally of special value for the study of the unconscious.

We have thus to distinguish clearly between the

two distinct stages that take place with most dreams before the disturbing stimulus results in a finished dream: the weaving of this stimulus into the terms of a repressed wish and the translation of the imagined wishfulfilment into imagery suitable for acceptance by consciousness. A little may be said about this second process, the *distortion* which makes the majority of dreams appear so absurdly unintelligible. The meaning of this distortion is a more difficult question, the answer to which was suggested above, but the fact itself of distortion is easy to ascertain. It is often quite patent, for instance, how a place or a person in a dream is made up by simply fusing two or more places or persons together as if on a composite photograph. More often elements are taken from each and fused together or elements common to both are abstracted. This mechanism of fusion is termed condensation. It holds good in both directions: one element in the manifest content of the dream may be connected with several in the latent content and vice versa, so that the analysis is like the unravelling of a network. Another one is displacement, whereby the accent of significance is transferred from where it originally belonged to a point of intrinsically less importance. The ideas of the latent content are usually dramatized, i. e., expressed in terms of action. Even at the moment of entering consciousness a further change occurs, called secondary elaboration, and this proceeds after waking so that a dream as remembered and written down at the time differs from one recollected later, a fact taken full account of in the analysis of dreams;

to this latter mechanism is due any feature of order or sense that the dream may possess.

It has been shown how the underlying thoughts "regress" to the infantile unconscious. They also regress in another sense of the word, back from their ideational form to the raw material of all thought, i. e., to sense imagery. This is preponderatingly visual in dreams, for a special reason, but occasionally other sense impressions, sound and smell, also occur. As may be expected in processes so closely connected with the unconscious, symbolism is often found in dreams, and, indeed, this is one of the chief fields in which it has been studied.

The majority of dreams when analyzed are seen to be concerned with material drawn both from current life and from infancy, hence the study of dreams affords an invaluable opportunity for investigating what is disturbing the deeper layers of the mind at any given moment and also the ultimate source (in early development) of the various emotional reactions connected with this. It is used clinically for both these purposes, the latter being naturally the more difficult to achieve. By means of it one can penetrate to the most primitive and intimate layers of the mind, and it is not surprising that the wishfulfilments met with there are invariably self-centred in nature, i. e., the wishes are entirely personal ones even when they refer to other people.

From the circumstance that most analysts are more occupied with the study of the unconscious than of dreams as such, using them merely for that purpose, it is perhaps natural that an impression should have been aroused justifying in part the frequent statement that "Freud says all dreams are sexual". In point of fact, however, in his theory there is no necessary connection at all between dreams and sexuality. The function of dreams, expounded above, has nothing to do with sexuality; the disturbing instigators of dreams may or may not be sexual in nature; the wishfulfilment by means of which the dream is constructed need not be sexual, though, it is true, it most often is.

CHAPTER V

ERRORS IN MENTAL FUNCTIONING

THIS CHAPTER is perhaps the most popular and least
unacceptable part of psychoanalysis, and, if carefully
studied, it is at the same time very instructive, for
the phenomena concerned are accessible to everyone
and are models for more complex problems. The
subject-matter is the numerous kinds of slips in the
mental functioning of everyday life, slips in the
tongue, slips of the pen, mislaying objects, and the
like. They may be classified as follows: A. *Motor*:
(1) making a mistake in carrying out an intended
purpose, whether in speech, writing, or any other
action; (2) carrying out an unintended purpose, "accidentally" doing something one had not really meant
to. B. *Sensory*: (1) simple failure, such as forgetting,
overlooking and the like; (2) erroneous perception,
an error in memory, in vision and so forth. Inasmuch
as these errors represent flaws in the normal functioning of the mind, they may be likened to minor neurotic symptoms and, indeed, investigation of them
shows that this resemblance is very considerable,
though, of course, far from complete. There are certain
features common to them all. Thus they are only

temporary disturbances of a function which at another time would be performed quite correctly, and the incorrectness is at once recognized as soon as attention is drawn to them. We usually attach no meaning to them and "explain" them, if at all, as being due to inattention, to chance, and so on.

Freud, on the contrary, has put forward the view that most of these happenings are really determined by mental processes of which the subject is at the moment unaware. It is an example of the way he has carried his belief in absolute determinism into minute, and often apparently trivial, matters. Interestingly enough, in this particular respect, he has only extended a conclusion which the natural intuition of mankind had already divined in part. For example, a man who has failed to appear at a rendezvous will seek in vain to be forgiven on the plea that he had forgotten about it—will, indeed, with this plea only increase the lady's resentment. Even if he falls back on the customary psychological explanations, and describes how urgent business had filled his mind, he will only hear in reply: "How curious that such things didn't happen last year! It only means that you think less of me." Similarly, when a man begins to be forgetful about paying accustomed attentions to his wife, overlooks her birthday, and so on, she correctly interprets it as a change in their relations. Another field in which we rarely fail to read significance into the mistake is that concerning our personal names. Few people can avoid feeling a twinge of resentment when they find that their name has been forgotten, especially if it is by someone from whom they had reason to expect or hope that it would be remembered. When a patient consulting me keeps addressing me as Dr. Smith, I am under no illusion about his private opinion of me.

Let us first take the simplest case. One aspect of Freud's repression theory, which was sketched above, is its application to the subject of memory. Leaving aside the vexed question of "bad memory" in general and confining ourselves to the simpler one of why a person should at a given moment forget a name or something else which he knows perfectly well, one must say that here is a failure in a mental function where there was no reason to anticipate it; we have, therefore, an unmistakable problem. According to Freud, there must in such a case be a definite motive for not wanting to remember; the motive may be entirely unconscious and in obvious contradiction to the desperate efforts the person is making consciously to revive the memory. The motive may be directly connected with the memory itself, such as when it is part of a train of unpleasant thoughts one does not wish to revive, or, more often, it is connected with some other idea or train of thought with which the memory in question happens to be associated. Forgetting is thus, strictly speaking, not a defect, but an act, though it is performed without the subject's knowledge. Psychoanalysis of each individual instance is able to disclose the particular motive at work. The same explanation has been found to hold good in two more extensive fields. All neuroses depend on amnesia, and in some cases of hysteria there can be massive losses of memory, extending even to the memory of the person's name, identity, and past life. Both here and in the more familiar field of infantile amnesia Freud has been able to show that the forgetting is really purposive, dictated by the motive to avoid some piece of self-knowledge. That we cannot recollect our memories of childhood, or only a small selection of them, in spite of our knowledge that that time was one rich in complicated mental experience, we are apt to take for granted as something not needing an explanation. This is one of the many examples of Freud's having investigated and explained phenomena where the very existence of the problem had hitherto been largely ignored.

One or two simple examples of suppression of intention may be quoted. When a person is unusually good at remembering to post letters, his forgetting to do so on a given occasion betokens some counter-will; this may be connected with the contents of the letter, a part of him being undecided about sending it, or something more indirectly associated with it, or mere annoyance at being asked to post it when he is in a hurry, all of which can only be ascertained by individual analysis. If, on the other hand, he has the common trait of being generally unreliable in posting letters it must mean that the idea of letters represents some more personal idea in his unconscious and that his attitude indicates a reluctance to part with some possession; this may or may not go together with a trait of meanness in general. An equally familiar case is that of the people who are notoriously bad at returning books they have borrowed; their convenient forgetfulness betrays a tendency to acquisition, which for a particular unconscious reason is specially apt to get connected with books, a tendency they may very well repudiate if taxed with it, and quite sincerely so.

A second group of such erroneous functioning is where one impulse interferes with another. The person consciously intends to say or write or do something, but some other impulse, of which he is either not aware at the moment or is totally unconscious of, takes advantage of some distraction, fatigue or concentration of attention to force its way through to expression. A patient who came to be treated for a morbid dread of infection said: "There have been several cases of fear in our district lately," when he meant "fever". What caused the slip was not, as philologists might maintain, the fact that the two words had so much in common (each consisting of two syllables, each beginning with "fe" and ending with "r"), but the fact that the word "fever" was strongly invested with the emotion of fear; it is as though he would rather talk about his fear which he hoped would be cured than about fevers of which he was really afraid. Every day of a psychoanalyst's work brings several examples of these slips, the interpretation of which is a helpful, and usually very easy, part of the analysis. The same is true of such "accidental" happenings as the mislaying or losing of objects, which are nearly always determined by some unconscious motive, however unlikely this may seem to the conscious mind whose attitude is quite the opposite.

A still more interesting group is that in which the person does not simply make a mistake in carrying out his intention, does something other than what he consciously intends to do, but where he involuntarily performs some act he had no conscious intention whatever of doing. We have here a scale ranging from the trivial occasions on which someone "accidentally" knocks over a glass of water to relieve some suppressed annoyance, to the tragic occurrences where death may be the result of some unconscious impulse that has involuntarily come to expression. Many collisions, train or motor-car smashes, climbing fatalities, and the like, are really brought about by an unwitting act which is the automatic expression of some unconscious impulse, perhaps of murder, suicide, or other suppressed tendency.

The reader must be referred to the literature on the subject for the analyses of examples and for the general bearings of the propositions here briefly indicated, notably on the problem of free will, but a word may be added on the general social significance of the processes under consideration. This is much greater than might perhaps be imagined, and for the following reason. It is certain that everyone, and more especially sensitive people, can intuitively interpret the meaning of these "slips" to a far greater extent than is consciously recognized and, what is more, that people then react to what they have unconsciously perceived through the other person's self-betrayal. Many misunderstandings in life arise, in short, from the very opposite, from a too good understanding. The first person accuses the second of some tendency or meaning which he has to rebut with the more heat because it is one the existence of which he is vigorously striving not to recognize in himself. It is well known that most family and marriage quarrels, even the most desperate, are over trifles, but it is just these trifles that have betrayed underlying attitudes and tendencies, the seriousness of which is not so disproportionate to the effects as the trifles themselves seem to the onlooker to be.

CHAPTER VI

DISORDERS OF MENTAL FUNCTIONING

THE importance of this branch of the subject is that it has always been, and probably always will be, the chief source of the data on which psychoanalytic conclusions are based. Nowhere else is there such an admirable magnifying lens as that presented by neurotic suffering or the opportunity to come to the closest quarters with the living facts themselves. Lenses distort as well as magnify, and a good deal of the doubt concerning psychoanalytic findings is due to their having been obtained from material that is thought to be both untrustworthy and abnormal. It is therefore necessary to say with emphasis that both these supposed deficiencies are of a very superficial kind; it would be true to say that on the whole they are apparent rather than real deficiencies. The question of trustworthiness belongs to the theme of psychoanalytic technique, which cannot be properly dealt with here. As to the abnormality, however, we may call attention to a few relevant considerations. The deviation from the so-called normal (incidentally, a state of affairs the present writer has never yet encountered) is throughout quantitative, not qualitative. Many of the symptoms of neurotic disorders may strike the average person at first sight as being alien to his imagination, but minor parallels for all of them can be found in everyday experience; they are little more than magnifications. And when one penetrates to the causal chain of which they are the final manifestation, one finds oneself at once on familiar ground. Indeed, the deeper one goes in this direction, the closer is the relation to the problems of normal development, and the harder does it become to specify what the essential distinctions between normal and abnormal are. We can make some approximations to the final truth, but we still cannot say precisely what it is that ultimately decides whether a given child will later develop nervous trouble or not.

It follows from these considerations that nervous disorders must be regarded in a much less "medical" light than is generally done. They are certainly not "diseases" in the accepted sense. They are rather one particular mode of reaction to difficulties in development that are part of the universal lot. All neuroses are the manifestation of difficulties in human relationships, so if one wishes to retain the word "disease", one will have to effect a distinction between ordinary medical complaints which represent a disordered relationship between the individual and his physical environment and neuroses which represent a disordered relationship between the individual and his human environment. The one is a part of the study of physiology, the other of sociology.

The point we are making can be applied by comparing the subject-matter of the present chapter with that of the previous one. No one would call a slip of the tongue a medical complaint, and, indeed, the only investigations of the matter that had been made before Freud were undertaken by philologists and, occasionally, by psychologists. Yet a slip of the tongue is undoubtedly in a sense a morbid phenomenon and represents a failure in the functioning of certain mental and physical machinery. More than this, close investigation shows that there is a far-reaching correspondence between the nature of the failure and that of neurotic manifestations. This is even more extensively true of dreams, the structure of which is quite astonishingly akin to that of neurotic symptoms, and no one has ventured to assert that dreams are not entirely normal occurrences.

We have not to do here with details of treatment of neurotic disorders or with their clinical aspects. It suffices to say in regard to the latter that there are two principal types, the hysterical and the obsessional neurosis respectively, and that the psychological mechanisms of the various types show important differences. The manifestations may be either positive, such as a pain or a tremor, or negative, such as a lack of a particular feeling or an inhibition of a particular capacity. They may be either physical, such as persistent vomiting or blindness, or purely mental, such as an intense fear or torturing obsession. These definite symptoms are at one end of a scale, at the other end of which the neurotic manifestations would seem, from a strictly medical point of view, very indefinite, though no less real, including such practical complaints as general intense unhappiness, inability to cope with family, marital, social, or professional situations.

Formerly these states were explained by the co-operation of two factors: Inherited weakness of the nervous constitution (a high-sounding but very empty phrase) and some current difficulty, of which disappointment in love and overwork were the most typical. Between these two Freud inserted a third, namely, the effect of certain experiences during the early sexual development. He in no way denied the significance of the other two; on the contrary, he has done much to define more nearly the essential nature of them and the exact continuity subsisting among all three. The course of events leading to a neurosis may shortly be described as follows. The combination of the two older factors, derived from heredity and from childhood respectively, yields a particular mental constitution which renders it difficult for the person to meet and cope with various exigencies of life. The latter are specific in each case, this depending on the precise constitution: one man can face death in battle, but not the making of an after-dinner speech; with another man the reverse would hold good. The situations thus found difficult or impossible may be either quite trivial in themselves (were it not for a special importance they acquire from their relation to the particular predisposition just mentioned), they may be what an average person would consider difficult (such as facing grief, bankruptcy, moral or physical dangers, and the like), or they may appear to be so general as to deserve the name of life itself; under the last heading would be grouped the cases where someone breaks down at certain critical ages or when faced with the ordinary responsibilities of grown-up life.

In such a situation the person destined to neurosis turns inwards, undergoes what is called "introversion", and develops a set of fantasies with the object of remedying or obliterating the real difficulty. These fantasies soon become associated with unconscious ones and a state of regression is brought about, the disturbance radiating into ever deeper and older layers of the unconscious. When the repressed part of the unconscious is in its turn reactivated, the impulses composing it come, of course, into conflict with the opposing repressing forces emanating from the ego. They have been stirred, however, and clamor for expression. Now, the manifestations of neurosis are nothing more nor less than the disguised expression of these repressed impulses, and the disguise is brought about in a very similar, though not quite identical, way to that described in an earlier chapter in connection with the formation of dreams. In a word, a neurosis is the external manifestation of an (unconscious) conflict between the most fundamental parts of the personality.

What is peculiar to the neuroses in contrast to the other phenomena considered earlier (slips and dreams) is, apart from their external appearance and practical significance, that the essential factors concerned are invariably sexual in nature. This does not hold good, of course, for the current instigator that sets in motion the process described above, but it does for both the factors that determine the specific predisposition and also for the energy that creates and sustains the nervous symptoms. According to psychoanalysis, the latter are simply disguised expressions of infantile sexuality. It is to be noted that they are never expressions of what is ordinarily called sexuality in the adult sense, a point which can easily lead to confusion. In the light of this statement, Freud's theory that the oedipus complex constitutes the kernel of every neurosis should become less unintelligible, if no less startling.

The discovery, now widely accepted even in non-analytic circles, that neurotic suffering is fundamentally due to unconscious conflicts, has been immensely useful in the matter of treatment, for this had to be purely empirical before anything was known about the pathology of the condition. It is now plain that there are only two possible ways whereby a cure of these troublesome disorders can be attempted. One, the most ambitious, is treatment by means of psychoanalysis, which makes both sides of the conflict conscious, and thus affords the opportunity for more satisfactory and less neurotic solutions being reached. An essential condition for the existence of a neurosis is unconsciousness of the causative factors; by psychoanalysis this essential condition is destroyed. What happens is that the blind repression maintained at the dictates of the childish superego (see the first chapter of this section) is replaced by conscious control exercised by the ego itself. All other methods of treatment really act, whatever their pretensions, by strengthening the superego through identification being unconsciously established between the idea of the physician and that of the parent from whom this superego was derived. There is a limit to what can be accomplished along these lines, for they afford no solution of the conflict, and the dependence on suggestive influence brings with it disadvantages of its own. This suggestive influence is, of course, also operative in psychoanalysis, but it is the very essence of what is analyzed and thus dissipated, for it proves to be identical with the morbid dependence on the childish superego.

APPLICATIONS OF PSYCHOANALYSIS

CHAPTER I

MEDICINE

THE medical profession has not yet appreciated the significance that psychoanalysis must have both for their technical problems and for their general outlook. Psychoanalysis will constitute a link of incalculable importance between medical and social problems, an aspect of the matter on which we need not enlarge. It happens also that the general attitude of psychoanalysis is in harmony with the newer points of view now being developed within medicine itself. By this we refer to the increasing tendency to direct attention to the functional aspects of the organism, to the practical question of how the body is actually functioning, rather than concentrating it on the anatomical state of various organs: in medical language, attention is being focussed on function instead of on lesions. This accords well with the point of view introduced by psychoanalysis, for this, with the stress it lays on active strivings, repressions, conflicts, and so on, is throughout a dynamic or functional one.

The field in which psychoanalysis most evidently overlaps medicine is that of the neuroses, one which has always been the despair of the profession, its greatest reproach, and the greatest opportunity for quacks. When one reflects that medical practitioners devote more than a thousand times as much time in their training to consideration of the body than they do to consideration of the mind, it is not at all surprising that so many of them find a difficulty in apprehending a problem in pathology in terms of psychology. The pressure to convert it somehow into a purely physical problem, to lay all the emphasis on whatever slight physical factors may be present, is almost overwhelming. It is therefore extremely difficult for the medical practitioner to form any just appreciation of the extraordinary scope of neurotic disorder even within the ordinary field of medicine. It is doubtful whether any group of bodily disorders is so common and far-reaching in its consequences as the neurotic one, apart altogether from its constant combination with the physical. Nevertheless, the estimate sometimes made that one-half of all suffering a doctor is called upon to treat is of neurotic origin is probably a considerable exaggeration.

The scant respect paid to psychology in medical education is, perhaps, not altogether unconnected with the way in which sexual problems are shirked there. Among the laity the impression prevails that doctors have occult knowledge of such matters, and sexual problems are often euphemistically referred to as "medical questions". They are astounded when they learn that such matters form no part whatever of medical education, that they are avoided in medical schools with the same meticulous care as in girls' schools, and that the practitioner is launched into the world as uninformed of them as any layman. Little wonder that he often finds it more convenient to pronounce oracularly that sexual factors are unimportant in disease than to repair the gap in his own education.

It is, of course, impossible to expect all medical practitioners to acquire special knowledge in this field any more than in any other branch of medicine, but they have so constantly to deal with situations dependent on psychological and sexual factors that some general notion of the problems involved would unquestionably be of value to them and their patients. It is in the field of prevention that, as perhaps elsewhere, their greatest opportunity lies. Often and often in the age of childhood or adolescence a sage word of advice would be of inestimable benefit for the individual's future happiness, and might obviate the necessity of treating a neurosis later on.

It is hard to discuss here the vexed question of the influence mental processes have on bodily functioning and the relation of this to bodily disease. One may, however, point out that when psychoanalysis insists on the importance of various instincts, sexual, hate, and so forth, in the production of suffering, it is insisting on factors which have a bodily as well as a mental aspect. Instincts, from the fact alone of their relation to tendencies inborn in the germ cell, are certainly in part bodily processes, and something is already known of the various chemical and physiological changes that accompany their activity. It is, indeed, plain that psychoanalysis is here performing a task of considerable theoretical interest in forging a link between bodily and mental studies. From this point of view such phrases as that "the mind acts on the body and causes disease in it" cease to be so repellent to our philosophical preconceptions. Evidence is certainly accumulating to show that a number of bodily disturbances, even those leading to permanent anatomical changes, may be brought about by factors which we have described above in terms of neurosis or unconscious mental conflict.

A third field of medicine should be mentioned here, one which occupies an intermediate position between the psychological and the physical—namely, that of insanity. Certain forms of insanity are undoubtedly caused by bodily infection, though even here the mental effects cannot be properly understood except by psychological study, to which psychoanalysis has already made interesting contributions. A much larger number, however, are of unknown origin, and there is naturally much debate about the relative importance of mental and bodily factors in their causation. The commonest of these is called dementia praecox; psychoanalysis has thrown much light on the genesis of its symptomatology and has been able to effect considerable improvement in early cases, without, however, claiming to have brought about radical cure of the condition. The most brilliant successes of psychoanalysis in this field have been with paranoia, or delusional insanity, and alternating, or manic-depressive, insanity (mania and melancholia). With both of these, psychoanalysis has put forward an. extensive theory of their genesis, one based on extremely detailed unravelling of a number of cases, and has been able to effect actual cures in selected cases.

CHAPTER II

EDUCATION

THE application of psychoanalysis to the understanding and upbringing of children holds more promise for the future than any other, but there are many pitfalls by the way. Some pedagogues, with more enthusiasm for the subject than genuine knowledge of it, have preached and attempted the application of it to school life in a way that no analyst can support, for there remains a great deal of work still to be done before we can feel sure of our ground here. This criticism is made not because the bearings of psychoanalysis on the problems of childhood are not important; on the contrary, it is because of their weighty import that one needs to be specially clear about them.

No extensive work has been done in psychoanalysis in regard to education in the sense of actual teaching, as distinct from general upbringing. But a great deal is known on the matter which comes to light in individual psychoanalytic work. Three points only will be selected by way of illustration. In the first place, the very act of teaching, of imparting information, is often unduly resisted by the child, in spite of its natural thirst for knowledge, because the child consciously or unconsciously takes it as constituting a criticism. The simple fact that the child's previous ignorance has to be implied, and that an endeavor is being made to remedy what is regarded as an undesirable state of affairs, often accompanied by an avowed effort to "improve" the child, is a definite wound to its selflove, and at times to still more obscure complexes. To the extent that this is so the child makes a bad learner, quite irrespective of its intellectual gifts. Children are deeply sensitive to anything resembling moral criticism, and one may lay down the proposition that the more moral a flavor is imparted into the teaching the greater is the inhibiting effect on the child's future intelligence. The deeper reason for this brings us to our second point. Teachers carry in the child's unconscious much of the significance formerly attaching to the parents. This is so not only superficially, in matters of authority, and the like, but also in respect to the deeper erotic ties; indeed, it is not at all uncommon for the latter to become evident particularly with girls, at some stage of the school career. Successful teaching depends altogether on the affective (feeling) bonds between teacher and pupil, probably on both sides. We know that there are many repressions and reactions in connection with the unconscious erotism in which these bonds originate, so that an actual relationship is made up of varying positive and negative attitudes. No theory of education can be complete that does not take into account these fundamental considerations. The third point concerns the actual subject-matter taught. The way in which this is assimilated shows, as is well known, extraordinary variations, and this not only in gross matters such as when a child is good at languages and hopeless at mathematics, but also within the details of each subject itself. These variations are at present ascribed to intellectual capacities or deficiencies, but psychoanalysis can show that in the majority of cases it is far more a question of affective inhibition versus sublimation, this depending on the child's reaction to the unconscious associations of the subject-matter. This may be evidenced in the finest details, for one has to remember that every part of the conscious topic becomes associated with unconscious ideas, and so can on occasion symbolize these. Not merely can all arithmetic become "difficult," i. e., unconsciously prohibited, because of the unconscious association "figures—counting on fingers—forbidden fingering", but errors in computation can be traced to such factors as a queer half-conscious preference for certain figures and dislike of others, this, in turn, being due to what they may symbolize. It constantly happens during psychoanalysis that a faculty in which the patient believed he was deficient is simply released by overcoming the repressions unconsciously connected with it. Experiences such as this make one profoundly distrustful of the fashionable intelligence tests, for the simple reason that what is tested is never the same with different children. There is here a virgin field waiting for research.

On the vast topic of upbringing there is far more to be said than on that of education proper, so that here again a small selection must be attempted. The outstanding point is that the young child is in the course of its development unconsciously struggling with conflicts of vital importance for its whole future. The significance of this may be estimated from the psychoanalytic conclusion that all character is permanently formed for good or ill by the age of five, later influences having only superficial effects or at most rearranging the elements already built. In these five years the child has to go through a complicated emotional development that it has taken mankind fifty thousand years to achieve, namely, the civilizing of his primary instincts. Reflection on this must increase one's tolerance for childish difficulties and misdemeanours and one's patience in dealing with them. Love is as necessary for a child's mental development as food is for its bodily development, and yet it has to be gradually weaned from certain manifestations of the love instincts. The more gently this necessary weaning is carried out, the more it is left to the child's nature to perform itself, the better can the child tolerate it and the less injurious its after-effects. The more a child's development comes about through its interests and affections rather than through moral training, the less sharp are the unavoidable conflicts and their consequences. Most children become over-moral without any assistance from the environment, though their demands in this respect tend to become more reasonable as the latency period progresses; and more naughtiness is due to a struggle with an over-guilty conscience than to any lack in this.

Next only to love and patience one would put

honesty in the order of importance in child upbringing. The common belief that the parent must pose as
a model of perfection to the child, at whatever cost to
truth, is more flattering to the parent's self-esteem than
beneficial to the child's development, and the corollary
that this can be accomplished only by suppressing all
knowledge of the deepest interests of life is certainly
deleterious to the latter. Without supporting the exaggerated claims sometimes asserted for sexual en-
lightenment as a panacea in child upbringing, an
analyst is bound to perceive the harmful effects of the
wilful dishonesty that still prevails in this matter.
Children instinctively know far more of the truth
about such things, either consciously or unconsciously,
than is generally supposed, and the real effect of en-
lightenment is not the imparting of information, but
the sanctioning of it. The benefit of this depends,
therefore, on the parent's attitude far more than on
what is actually said.

All children appear to pass through a stage of
neurosis. Whether this is inevitable even with wiser
upbringing, we do not know. Nor is it possible to
predict the extent to which the child will spontaneous-
ly overcome the neurotic stage, or at what cost in later
inhibition or predisposition to adult neurosis. The
attempt has therefore been made to render the path
of development more secure and less painful by analyzing the young child. Mrs. Melanie Klein, a pupil
of two of Freud's most distinguished co-workers, Drs.
Abraham and Ferenczi, has developed a special technique for this purpose. Although we have had as yet

only a few years' experience of this work, the results so far have been most promising and instructive, and the present writer is convinced that in the future an important part of therapeutic analysis, perhaps the most important part, will lie in this sphere. It is indispensable, however, that such an analysis be a real one, quite independent of any educative measures.

CHAPTER III

ANTHROPOLOGY

THERE are two points of connection between this chapter and the preceding one. The first rests on a new version of the equation often established between child and savage, the other on the predominantly genetic interest of the two themes.

When psychoanalysis comments on certain resemblances between the mentality of the child and that of the savage, it does so without implying, as is usually so, any depreciation of the latter. The reason for this is that psychoanalytic work inculcates a much greater respect for the child's mind than generally prevails, for it shows that it is far more complicated and less unlike the adult mind than is supposed. On the other hand, it establishes an unusually sharp distinction between two types of thinking, illustrated at their extreme by conscious logical thought and unconscious associative thought. The distribution of these two types is not so closely correlated with the age of the individual as might be imagined, though it is true that, on the whole, the one is more manifest in the adult and the other in the child. Similarly it is undeniable that the unconscious type, sometimes not very aptly termed prelogical thinking, is more easily recognized among savages than among ourselves, and this, in spite of their possessing logical faculties perhaps equal to our own. Many interesting examples of their thought, in their superstitions, magical beliefs, and so on, we can readily perceive are determined by emotion rather than by reason, and an amazingly close connection can be established between them and the phenomena studied by psychoanalysis in particularity among children.

It is unfortunately not possible here even to illustrate the far-reaching correspondence just alluded to between the emotional fantasy life of savages and children, and we must confine ourselves to a few generalizations that have emerged from the many detailed studies of it that have been made. Such studies have been of mutual interest to psychoanalysis and to anthropology. On the one hand, the detailed investigation of the unconscious has enabled psychoanalysts to proffer explanations of many baffling problems in anthropology, such as the horror of incest, mother-right, couvade, taboo, initiation ceremonies, totemism, and so forth, while on the other hand, the material and connections displayed in anthropological data have confirmed the findings of psychoanalysis and given them a broader basis. We learn in this way that many elaborate institutions, ritualistic practices, social customs and beliefs, and so forth, are complicated outcomes of the endeavor to deal with the very same unconscious conflicts that trouble our children and produce the neuroses which form the main subject-matter of psychoanalytic work. The bearing of this correlation on comparative sociology and anthropology is necessarily great, for in the study of individual neuroses we have an opportunity to check our conclusions and submit them to a fine analysis that is unequalled in those more massive spheres.

Freud has drawn an interesting parallel between the fantasy life of neurotics and of savages, and on the basis of this and more detailed work by other investigators differences between the two have been elucidated that are as interesting for comparative work as the correspondence mentioned above. Savages as a whole resemble our neurotics, as contrasted with the more normal civilized man, in having a large part of the mind that has been imperfectly transformed in the course of development, one that is merely a disguised and not an altered unconscious. In other words, both are nearer to the primary instincts and primitive modes of thought, and are to a greater extent dominated by the pleasure-principle. Affection and friendliness are more impeded by the closeness of the opposite tendencies of hate and hostility; the attitude in human relationships is more ambivalent, as it is called. They have both of them overcome much less of the fear and guilt that lie so deeply rooted in man. In consequence they are much more moral, though often in an irrational way. A feature that leads us to the second of the two points mentioned at the beginning is that the neurotic life of savages is far more systematically organized on social lines than it is among civilized peoples. In the latter there has been more smoothing over and rationalizing of the unconscious conflicts, so that the neurotic manifestations of them displayed by individual sufferers are treated as disturbing intrusions into an otherwise orderly scheme of society.

This consideration gives some clue to the past development of civilization. Without, of course, maintaining that civilized peoples have passed through stages of culture resembling that of any living savages, which would be a very crude and inaccurate view, we can say that, on the whole, savages (together with neurotics and children) show many indications of the earlier stages of development through which in one form or another all mankind must have passed. Just as the body, especially in its developmental stages, shows traces of earlier phases in the evolution of mankind, so may the unconscious be regarded as in some respects a repository of the past experiences in the early mental development of mankind. The actual relation of this to the problems of heredity is a very vexed question, which cannot be regarded as in any way settled, though Freud himself inclines to the belief in direct inheritance of mental processes. However this may be, there is much evidence to show that the study of the unconscious can contribute data to be estimated together with other data in forming conclusions on man's remote past. In an important study of totemism (indications of which, by the way, still crop up among our neurotics), which has been supplemented in a still more detailed work by a distinguished anthropologist, Dr. Roheim, Freud has made it probable that this extensive institution is in great part an elaborate defense against the oedipus complex (incest and cannibalistic father-murder). Following hints put forward by Darwin and Atkinson, he has developed the view that this complex, in the form of the fight between the "old man of the tribe" and the younger males, played a vital part in the foundation of social and, ultimately, civilized life. Indeed, to the reactions of remorse and fear surrounding it he traces the beginnings of all law, morality, and religion. So far-reaching has been the work that started in the treatment of hysterical pains!

A new school of anthropologists, the "diffusionists", who attach great importance to the spread of culture from a limited centre, are under the curious illusion that their views are incompatible with the conclusions of psychoanalysis, on the score that the latter lay great stress on similarities among the different races and cultures of mankind. In reality, there is no such incompatibility, for their work deals with a superficial layer of the mind, and the analytical with the deepest and most primitive layers, with the instincts and the biological reactions to them which certainly have much in common in all people.

CHAPTER IV

SOCIOLOGY AND POLITICS

SOCIAL institutions and law-making are concerned partly with material welfare, economic, hygienic, and so forth and perhaps to a still greater extent with more ideal values such as prestige, honor, patriotism, class and sex conflicts, theories of government, ideas of justice, regulation of moral conduct, and so on. It is evident that subjective factors must enter into the second group even more extensively than they do into the first, but they are, in any event, never lacking. It may safely be said that psychoanalysis would be able to throw light on any one of them by pointing to unconscious factors influencing judgment. According to psychoanalysis, the greater part of the mental energy that goes to these various interests is derived from the more primary tendencies of the unconscious, either in the form of sublimations that transform the energy into these interests or in the form of complicated institutions, especially moral and religious ones, whose ultimate aim is to keep the primitive tendencies in check. Analysis of the real meaning of the processes in question gives a far more favorable opportunity for thinking freely and objectively on the problems at issue.

The subject of health, for example, is surrounded by endless superstitions, fears, and taboos, which are by no means confined to the laity. Even in the most material field, that of economics, psychoanalysis has shown that it is rare for anyone to think freely and behave "normally" where money is concerned. One of the most surprising discoveries of psychoanalysis was that the idea of money is frequently a direct symbol of that of bodily dirt in the unconscious, and that the various complicated reactions to do with the latter idea constantly influence conscious judgments about money matters. To mention a single example, it was possible for a psychoanalyst to publish a prediction early in the first World War that after it had ended Great Britain would suffer acutely from unemployment because of an unduly hasty desire to return to the gold standard, a conclusion which even yet orthodox financiers refuse to perceive.

Free association of ideas takes us to the subject of war itself, certainly one of the gravest sociological problems. Here psychoanalytic investigations have shown the complexity of the factors concerned and the impossibility of radically coping with them unless their unconscious roots are thoroughly examined and understood. Compared with comprehensive study of this kind, the present vague propaganda of exhortations to denounce war are but pitiful fumblings, about the efficacy of which few serious thinkers are deceived.

The theory of government, again, about which the world is so despairingly divided at present, is a problem that intimately depends on the relation between child and parent, of which that between governed and governing is a magnification. To take the crudest illustration: psychoanalysis observes every day that the prodigious interest taken by the populace, with few exceptions, in the most banal doings of members of the British Royal Family proceeds from an unconscious identification between them and the individual's own family; the one is simply the glorification of the other along the lines of childish fairytales and fancies. The King is one of the most regular unconscious symbols for the father, the Queen for the mother, and so on. In Great Britain, we have a rather happy arrangement whereby the ambivalent attitude towards the father is dealt with by dividing his public representative into two persons. The head of the executive, the Prime Minister, is periodically cast from power and politically annihilated, while the respect due to the father is reserved for another person. The exaggerated claims on the Government to solve all problems and relieve all helplessness, with the corresponding manifestations of bitterness and disappointment, are continuations of the belief in the allpowerful father of childhood. The great question of leadership, the extent to which the general population can ever be expected to attain independence, i. e., an adult attitude, are ultimately problems of individual psychology.

Since it has fallen to the lot of psychoanalysis to elucidate the complexities of the sexual instinct to a greater extent than any other, it will not be surprising to learn that it is in a position to make many weighty contributions to the social problems relating to this instinct. The muddled thinking to be witnessed everywhere over the ramifications of the marriage question, the problems of divorce, birth control and eugenics, the endless unhappinesses and complications arising between the sexes, is a direct product of the unsolved conflicts that surround the earliest development of the sexual instincts, for the reactions proceeding from these conflicts are the foundation of all later attitudes.

We see nowadays many signs of revolt against the institution of the family, in spite of the familiar sociological dictum that the family is the basis of all society. How true is this dictum, and to what extent is it consistent with the possibilities of human nature to modify the institution so as to preserve the valuable components and discard the harmful ones? One can safely say that no adequate answer to fundamental questions such as these will be forthcoming without the help that psychoanalysis is able to afford.

CHAPTER V

CRIMINOLOGY AND LAW

THE topic that most concerns us here is that of moral responsibility. The controversy between doctors and lawyers over criminal responsibility is an old one. The former usually come off worse in the argument because they have to accept the lawyers' premises unchallenged and get led on into vain attempts to define a legal fiction in terms of reality. On the assumption that mental states and impulses of a certain kind are caused only by "disease" or "sin", two equally vague conceptions in this context, doctors are asked to discriminate nicely between the two, and they naturally tend to flounder badly in the process. The underlying theory appears to be that the law permits some modes of conduct to be caused, i. e., by disease, but not others. The latter are said to be the product of free will, which is omnipotent enough to create the first link in a chain of thought or conduct. By accepting a particularly arbitrary distinction between mental health and disease, doctors pass beyond the facts of their own science, and by accepting the legal view of free will they abandon the only fundamental canon of all science.

Psychoanalysis has many positive contributions to make on this subject, apart from the critical ones just indicated; the latter are necessarily pointed because psychoanalysis owes its very existence to a whole-hearted application of scientific determinism. The irrationality of the conduct in most cases of criminality would alone make one suspect the presence of unascertained factors in the depths of the personality, and there exists much direct evidence pointing to the same conclusion. The work that has been done, particularly abroad, with regular criminals has shown the complexity of the problems, which is largely due to the tangled deformation of character so often present. The point can be more simply presented by taking such a case as kleptomania, where the irrationality of the motivation, i. e., when the wealthy person throws away the stolen reel of cotton, is often beyond all question. Psychoanalysis is able to demonstrate in such cases that the impulse owes its uncontrollable force to the imperious necessity of assuaging some quite unconscious painful situation. The conduct is dictated by the need to relieve the tension brought about by conflict between some repressed impulse, which the crime symbolizes, and the intolerable sense of guilt accompanying it. Indeed, the impulse to commit some crime, even a serious one, so as to allay the guilt arising from the unconscious wish to commit an even more forbidden one represents a by no means infrequent mechanism; it is one of the many unexpected discoveries of psychoanalysis in this field.

The fact that psychoanalysts of necessity adopt a deterministic attitude towards the question of moral responsibility has led some unthinking critics to attribute to them a total repudiation of punishment, a view which no analyst has, in fact, expressed. The whole question of punishment, both in this field and in that of education, is badly in need of psychological investigation, which is all that any analyst could ask for. It is at all events plain that in the present system of legal punishment the deterrent and reformatory motives commonly put forward often cover the deeper motive of retribution. If the former were the main one there would at once be instituted a serious scientific investigation into the preventive efficacy of the various forms of punishment. Similarly with the second ground adduced: so long as the problem is viewed as a moral and not a psychological one, so long will the moral attitude of the law-maker and administrator mask the full psychological motives. Psychoanalysis can reveal the nature of the fear that underlies the tendency to revenge, and this has much more to do with people's apprehension at the immoral tendencies in their own unconscious than with dread of criminals. Intolerance of other people's wrongdoing is a sure sign of an uneasy conscience, of the effort it is costing to suppress forbidden unconscious tendencies.

The indignation displayed by most people at any threatened contact between law and psychology (not to mention the use of such words as psychoanalysis and the unconscious) is, in fact, well founded, for any attempt to investigate and understand the problems of human nature in question would probably entail a considerable revolution in the present methods and attitude of the law.

CHAPTER VI

ART AND LITERATURE

THIS subject has a special interest for psychoanalysts
on account of the widespread illusion that aesthetics
and psychoanalysis are in some way incompatibles.
No patient endowed with aesthetic feeling ever fails to
express the fear, often a morbidly intense one, that
this capacity will be destroyed in the course of the
analytic procedure.

Psychoanalysis has actually contributed much
more to the psychology of the artist than to that of art
itself, but it is impossible to separate the two problems. The first difficulty is that many quite disparate
things pass under the name of art. It is clear, for example, that much beautifying is of a purely decorative
nature, being ultimately derived from the same (ex-
hibitionistic) impulses as those underlying personal
ornamentation. Again, the fondness to reproduce some
external object as faithfully as possible has far more
relation to the imitative instinct than to any true
aesthetic feeling, though doubtless the manipulative
capacities acquired through exercising this instinct are
of value in the technique of the artist's craftsmanship.
Nor can aesthetic feeling be completely identified with

the sense of beauty, for it appears in some instances to transcend this. There is wide agreement nowadays that its essence resides in an impersonal but pleasurable contemplation of various formal relations, whether in visual outline, color, sound, or ideas.

On going into the matter psychologically, the first thing one observes is a peculiarly strong repudiation of the possibility that true aesthetic feeling is concerned with anything more than form. Extreme purists even maintain that any content there may be in good art is simply a concession to the weaker public, an inducement for them to take an interest in the aesthetic qualities of the work. Just as any propaganda or moral purpose is held to vitiate an artistic play or novel, so is the hint of any ideational theme regarded as a blemish on the purity of artistic purpose in a picture or symphony. Aesthetic feeling must be kept uncontaminated by any such worldly motives as the desire to express what may be called human feelings. It is a thing in itself which has no connection with any biological instincts. According to psychoanalysis, the artist is here right in his attitude, but wrong in his conclusions. Detailed psychoanalysis of individuals shows that the aesthetic capacity and the artistic impulse proceed from peculiarly deep layers of the unconscious—indeed, the sense of inspiration itself signifies this—and that they represent one particular mode of dealing with the primordial conflicts existing in these layers. The artist's unconscious endeavor is to transmute in a particular direction the emotions arising from these conflicts and to express them in a pure aesthetic form. In this process there are some very special features that are in large measure peculiar to the artist's mentality.

The artistic impulse is far from being only an endeavor to gratify a particular form of pleasure; it also assuages pain. Keats' lines,

"And they shall be accounted poet kings
Who simply tell the most heart-easing things,"

were certainly not meant to be applied in a pretty sense only. It is part of the artist's gift to be able mysteriously to transform repellent or distressing themes into a form that is actually pleasurable. This is most striking in the case of tragedy, on which Aristotle founded his famous theory of catharsis. It would seem that a great part of the relief experienced, by both the artist and the spectator, has to do with the conviction of *inevitability*. This thesis, so evident with tragedy, can be extended to all forms of art. The attribute of certainty, and if possible perfection, the justness of the formal relationship that evokes aesthetic feeling—all this provides a refined kind of security to certain minds. The ultimate nature of this security and the reason why there is need for it, such questions can only be answered by study of the unconscious. We meet here another aspect of what was referred to earlier as the allaying of unconscious tension.

It is with literature that the whole problem is most accessible to psychological approach. No one would maintain that the formal elements of poetry, such as metre, suitably sounding words, and, above all, rhythm, absolutely indispensable as they are, could ever constitute the whole of poetry. There have to be ideas as well, and much of the aesthetic pleasure is derived from the sense of order and relationship in the presentation of these ideas. But these ideas do not stand alone: they are, in their turn, the representatives of unconscious ideas which are accessible to psychoanalysis. Many intensive studies of individual poets have been made on these lines, and the results are unequivocal in deciding the main question—namely, whether the artistic impulse is something apart from the rest of life or simply a highly special product of the same unconscious conflicts that manifest themselves in such a variety of ways. To mention a single point, Otto Rank, in his detailed monograph on the subject, was able to show that the themes in great literature, just as is well known to be so with fairytales, games, jokes, and many other products of the imagination, are innumerable variants of a relatively few fundamental *motifs*. Among these the different aspects of the incest motif, the derivatives of the oedipus complex, occupy an unexpectedly prominent position.

CHAPTER VII

MYTHOLOGY, FAIRY-TALES, FOLK-LORE, AND SUPERSTITION

AN immense amount of psychoanalytic work has been published on these fascinating subjects. As with anthropological material, problem after problem, however obscure previously, can be solved once one has the key to the unconscious motivations, and, on the other hand, the study of the material, which comes from such diverse sources and is presented objectively and impersonally, is both confirmatory and instructive. Many examples of typical symbolism, for instance, the genesis of which is often hard to understand in the study of individuals, becomes comprehensible when seen in the general social setting of mythology and folk-lore. Common to the whole group of phenomena included under the title of this chapter is the fact that they are all products of human fantasy, the investigation of which has been one of the main tasks of psychoanalysis. The part played in mythology by intellectual curiosity about astronomy, for example, was vastly over-estimated some years ago, and it is now widely recognized that we have to do with emotions about much nearer human concerns.

The psychoanalysis of myths shows clearly that they represent in a disguised way the most primitive wishes and fears of mankind. The mechanism of the disguise, as also the motive for it, is extremely similar to that of dreams, and, indeed, many mythologists before Freud had pointed out the far-going resemblances between dreams and myths. The energies that could not be transmuted into the real tasks and interests of life were expressed in the wishfulfilments of myths, and still more openly in that of fairy-tales. The higher religions emancipated themselves from their early mythological nature both by their concern about the affairs of real life and by their higher ethical achievements.

In the more religious variety of myth, notably in those of Egypt and Greece, the family nature of their content is manifest, and its shocking character stands in strange contrast not only to our own ideals of family life, but in all probability to those of the same people who believed the myths. It is not too much to say that the chief themes are those of incest and castration; every variety of murder and sexuality within the family is represented. But these are themes characteristic of the infantile life that persists in the adult unconscious, from which they very rarely emerge to the surface. Nowadays the same themes would be expressed, not in a mythical belief, but in a neurosis. The figures of the myths are thus glorified substitutes for members of the individual family.

In the other kinds of myth, those that pass insensibly into the form of legend, there is a more extensive disguise of the same primary material. A favorite motif, for instance, is identical with what is so often found in the analysis of early childhood life, namely, the changeling theme. The child expresses its dissatisfaction with its parents by repudiating its relationship with one or both, imagining that it is of higher birth, that it comes of kinder and more ideal parents, and it weaves various stories in which its inhibited wishes come to plain gratification. This is part of what Freud has called the "family romance" of children, an important part of their fantasy life. We met another indication of it in Chapter IV in connection with the Royal Family. It will be remembered that this was one of the features in the very legend from which the term "oedipus complex" was borrowed. In short, the fulfillment of unconscious wishes furnishes the main creative force in the formation of myths and fairy-tales.

The simplest superstitions are the familiar ones in which a particular act, such as spilling salt or walking under a ladder, is felt to be lucky or unlucky. We say "felt", for there are conventional superstitions that are not really believed in. When there is any feeling that there may perhaps "be something" in them, it is certain that an associative connection has been forged in that person's mind between the act and some unconscious idea. The unconscious idea in question is almost always the same with different people, for the connection belongs to the group of typical, i. e., well-nigh universal, symbols. Most of these superstitions, therefore, are easy to interpret from some knowledge of symbolism. Some such acts are vaguely lucky, others unlucky; most frequently the same act brings now good luck, now bad luck, according to the age, country, or context in which it occurs. In both cases the point is that the particular act is felt to be mysteriously significant. The explanation is that the act in the unconscious, which is symbolized by the trivial conscious one, is one of forbidden pleasure: the bad luck is, in the unconscious, the punishment for this pleasure, the good luck is the enjoyment of the pleasure without punishment. The punishment can sometimes be averted by propitiatory or reassuring acts such as "touching wood", which are, of course, also symbolic. These secondary acts of reassurance constitute the main content of some superstitions, e. g., the Southern European ones about the evil eye.

In more elaborate forms of superstition the idea of bad luck gets less vague, though it is not often precisely specified. It mostly refers to loss of money or injury to physical health. Detailed analyses have been published of many of these, e. g., the former beliefs in witchcraft, werewolves, and so forth. There is a transition between mental attitudes of this sort, which we now recognize as morbid, and numerous beliefs, such as that draughts are injurious to health, that tonics are good for the nerves, and so on indefinitely, where the superstitious nature of the belief is not yet acknowledged. How many of our beliefs are influenced by the mechanism of unconscious wishfulfillment (we all know that the wish is father to the thought consciously, but the range of the unconscious is incomparably greater), or, put otherwise, what share does illusion take in our judgment of reality? These are questions that open up a vast topic of obvious practical importance.

CHAPTER VIII

RELIGION

THE considerations of the preceding chapter bring us inevitably to the most delicate topic of all—that of religious beliefs. In general, psychoanalysis, being a branch of science, must, in common with all scientific thinking, endeavor to distinguish between beliefs based on verifiable evidence and those largely independent of such evidence or in contradiction to it. But it has, in addition, two special contributions to make on the subject of theology, one of a general psychological nature and one specific.

The first contribution is the evidence it can bring to show the extent to which apparently intellectual operations are influenced by unconscious processes, especially when they concern matters of great personal moment. Once mental processes of this kind are built up, the resulting product can be given a philosophical, spiritual, and intellectual façade which would impose itself as the whole structure. Conclusions formed in this way may or may not coincide with external reality, but their internal coherence is in itself no guarantee that they will.

The second contribution consists in a detailed

application of this principle. The subject of religious beliefs compels investigations in many individual analyses, so that much knowledge has accumulated about their genesis and unconscious correlates. In addition, many exhaustive analyses have been made of the psychological significance of various religious beliefs, on the basis of theological and anthropological material examined analytically. A short account may be given of some of the more generally important conclusions thus reached.

The theological statement that God is our Father appears to be fully justified in a psychological sense. Both militant atheism and devout belief in God can be equally traced to the child's earliest reactions to his earthly father (or to the idea of a father when the actual one is missing). The attributes of omnipotence, omniscience, and moral perfection are invariably ascribed to the father at one stage or another during the young child's growth; they proceed at least as much from internal necessities as from any external example or suggestion. Various repressions to do with the idea of the father, together with his obvious shortcomings when judged by so absolute a standard, lead to the attributes of perfection being abstracted from him and incorporated in an intangible figure. This, in a couple of words, is perhaps the gist of the mass of knowledge we possess about the complicated development of the idea of Godhead.

Over and over again the religious systems of the world have culminated in the worship of a Trinity, which has almost always consisted of the primordial figures of Father, Mother, Son. It can be shown in detail that the various beliefs and legends relating to these figures are throughout related to the unconscious conflicts that have to do with the members of the individual human family. In the Christian religion the figure of the Mother has been partly replaced by that of the Holy Ghost, but the change has been effected from motives which are accessible to investigation.

All religion is founded on the idea of sin, i. e., the sense of guilt at not reaching a prescribed standard. Without this idea religion loses all meaning. All sin can be expressed in terms of disobedience to the Father (or even rebellion against Him), or else desecration of the Mother (and her attributes or substitutes). Now these are the two components of the primal oedipus complex of childhood; incidentally, the Protestant and Catholic types of mind correspond with the component on which the accent falls. The subject of guilt has had to be investigated by psychoanalysis in very great detail, for it plays an important part in every individual analysis; the problems of neurosis, for example, are inseparable from those of guilt. A distinction can be drawn between childish guilt and its normal development into the adult conscience in which is incorporated all our moral and ethical standards; one speaks also of an aesthetic and scientific conscience. This normal conscience is the heir of the oedipus conflict of childhood. On the other hand, it commonly happens that errors in early development may prevent the normal evolution from taking place. Then there remains an excessive sense of guilt in the unconscious which is infantile and irrational in character and often morbid in its effects. The precise relation of the sin of religion to these two forms of guilt is too delicate a question for the answer to be given in a word. One can only say here that the lofty sense of spiritual value attaching to religious feeling and beliefs owes much of its importance to the fact that these at the same time fulfill the deepest cravings of the human mind and afford some appeasement to the unconscious moral tension. It is therefore not surprising that for many people they come to represent by far the most precious thing in life.

The other important element of religious beliefs, namely, that in an after-life, displays the feature of wishfulfillment more prominently than that just considered. Salvation betokens a joyful reunion with the parents against whom the unconscious sinful thoughts were directed. Heaven is the reward of that "at-one-ment." All the unsatisfactoriness, hardships, and injustices of this life will find their due compensation there. And it is fitting that the symbolism of heaven should contain endless allusions to the unconscious identification of this reward with the notion of recapturing a form of bliss that we once possessed (hence also the idea of the Fall), of returning to "that imperial palace whence we came".

To sum up: religious beliefs, whether savage, mythological or Christian, may or may not be true—in their nature they are not capable of proof or disproof—but it is highly probable that they would have arisen in their identical forms whether they were true

or not; the genesis of them can be adequately accounted for without invoking any external (supernatural)
agency. If one desired to apply psychoanalytic conceptions somewhat fancifully, one might say that mythological beliefs represent on the plane of social organiza-
tion the stage of childhood neurosis in the development of mankind, while much of religious belief similarly represents that of adolescent neurosis. But we
must not forget that neurosis is an expression of the
same forces and conflicts that have led to the loftiest
aspirations and profoundest achievements of our race,
and that neurotics are often the torch-bearers of civilization. They may strain themselves in the effort, but
without that effort there would be no civilization.

CONCLUSION

I⊤ would have been easy to present the principles of psychoanalysis in so general a way as to avoid producing the startling impression which many of the concrete statements in this book must make. In choosing the alternative the author has not refrained from presenting in a necessarily bald and perfunctory manner conclusions which he is aware must at times appear grotesquely crude. He has published elsewhere, it is true, detailed studies on all the topics dealt with here, to which the reader may be referred; but the reason why the present course was decided on was because so much misapprehension prevails on the subject that he wished to leave the reader in no doubt about what psychoanalysis really is. The reader is naturally not thereby put into a position to pass judgment on the subject, but at least he has been informed what psychoanalysis is about. The essence of Freud's discovery is his exploration of the unconscious, a concept which before his work was an empty term. Bound up with this is the mechanism of repression and the significance of infantile sexuality. From this proceeds the generalization that the child's later character, his future interests, happiness, and to a large extent his capacities are all principally dependent on his early reactions to his intimate relations with the family. On the manner in which he attempts to solve the unconscious conflicts in this sphere will depend the most important elements of his future life. Psychoanalysis is therefore essentially a genetic psychology. It traces the evolution of our primordial instincts into the elaborate patterns of our conscious activities. Darwin established the continuity between man's body and the rest of life on this earth: Freud has done the same for the human mind.

The outstanding conclusion to which we seem impelled is that the findings of psychoanalysis are either untrue or else they are of momentous import. One thing is certain and that is that they are not half-true. It is, of course, easier to adopt the first of the two possibilities, for one is thereby spared much painful thought. But the massive evidence now accumulated, drawn from the most diverse fields, and added to by constant daily experience, makes it increasingly difficult to maintain this comforting solution, and, indeed, it can be done only by avoiding first-hand experience of the problems.

The view of man's past and present seen in the perspective of psychoanalytic knowledge confirms that presented to us by biological consideration of him as a species, which is that he is still in the early stage of his development. The new organ he acquired of consciousness, or rather consciousness of self, has carried him far, but we are beginning to perceive its possible limitations. The teaching of psychoanalysis is that these are imposed by the nature of the unconscious and its relations to consciousness. The unquestionably imperfect manner in which he has hitherto dealt with the fundamental conflicts and disharmonies in the unconscious, from which emanates the energy of the whole mind, hampers him in a thousand ways, with the result that only a tithe of his potentialities are at his disposal.

It is commonly predicted that the advance of physical science, if continued at its present rate, will soon reduce mankind to the position of children playing with loaded pistols. It is at all events certain that man's power over his material environment, even though it be so unevenly applied as it now is, has far outstripped his control over himself. The future may very well show that to acquire this control, to render as available the unconscious as the conscious mind, shall mark an era in man's history as momentous as the achieving of consciousness was. The aim of psychoanalysis is no less than to render this possible.

ADDENDUM (1947)

Although nearly twenty years have elapsed since this book was first drafted I find on re-reading it little that needs changing. There was of course very much that could have been added to what was after all only a sketch of the elements of psychoanalysis and there is much more now. I must confine myself here to indicating the modern trends and problems of psychoanalytic research into the old contrasts between inborn and environmental factors in the production of human character and personality. Freud interpolated a third, intermediate one: the inner fantasy life of the infant, itself a product of congenital and early environmental influences. Workers had always oscillated in apportioning the significance due to these internal and external factors, and in present-day psychoanalytic research some concentrate more on the former, some more on the latter.

Work on the internal factors, deepening our knowledge of the early fantasy life of the infant, has mostly been carried out by London psychoanalysts, among whom the name of Melanie Klein is prominent. After elaborating a special technique for psychoanalyzing young children she and the group around her, notably Paula Heimann, Susan Isaacs, Joan Riviere, and Drs. Scott and Winnicott, were able to illumine the early inner life of infants much more fully than had previously been possible. Her conclusions have met with considerable criticism in London itself and will no doubt in the future meet with more elsewhere. This criticism is essentially a doubt about her assertions that complex mental processes, including the formation of the oedipus complex and the superego, take place at an earlier age than Freud has supposed, in the first two years of life instead of in the fourth or fifth. She has also laid great stress on the savagery of the infant's early impulses towards its parents and describes fantasies of tearing, devouring, and so on that remind one of the wilder Walt Disney films. My own work is in substantial accord with Mrs. Klein's findings, although I do not always agree with the theoretical formulations she has founded on them. Her work has in important ways affected the technique of adult analysis inasmuch as it has made clear the deepest impulses and fantasies of infantile origin which live on in the adult unconscious. She has also extended her investigations to the field of insanity and has thrown much light on the genesis of melancholia, paranoia, and schizophrenia. Her work inevitably has an important bearing on the problems of child upbringing, and the direct observations by Merril Middleton and others have shown without doubt that even slight variations in the matter of feeding, particularly at the breast, may exert an unsuspected influence on the later development of the individual. The inevitable frustrations of infancy stimulate aggressive responses, and a good deal of the subsequent development consists of various secondary reactions to, and defenses against these dreaded tendencies. The child's fear of itself is of cardinal importance for its destiny, and leads not only to the innumerable forms of inferiority (with subsequently various covers for this), but also accounts for the alternation between dependence and assertiveness so distressing in our social, and even political, life. Morality itself is probably generated as an aid in combating these deep fears, but unfortunately it takes to begin with—in the form of the superego—extremely harsh and cruel shapes, so that in the long run the moral attitudes are far from being as purely beneficient to civilization as they are popularly supposed to be.

At the other extreme from this line of investigation is that pursued particularly in certain American circles, with whom the name of Karen Horney is to be associated. Here stress is laid on the effect of various social institutions in moulding the development of the child. It is maintained that the manifold variations of these in the world affect the child's development itself. Malinowski, a famous English anthropologist, even maintained that an oedipus complex could arise only in a patriarchal society and not in a matriarchal one, but the present writer has pointed out serious fallacies in these conclusions. The extreme of this line is reached in the Marxian view that all human developments are essentially a super-structure dependent on the all-important factor of the economic mode of production in a given community. It is evident that these sociological factors enormously influence the modes of human activity and the manifold ways in which human nature expresses itself in different circumstances. It remains, however, to be shown how it is possible for these cultural influences to affect the deeper fantasies of the infant, or indeed to reach the unconscious at all. On the one hand, therefore, the high claim sometimes made for the ability of social institutions to modify fundamental traits in human nature are more than suspect, but on the other hand there is little doubt that these institutions can extensively affect the various ways in which these traits are outwardly manifested.

Valuable work has been done in the United States on what are nowadays termed psychosomatic conditions, and the names of Jelliffe and Alexander will always be associated with pioneering investigations of these conditions. By a psychosomatic state is meant a physical condition, usual with definite physical changes, which has been induced either partly or wholly by emotional fantasies and conflicts. Many physicians have for some time surmised this possibility, but they did not have the psychoanalyst's technical knowledge of the emotional factors to be able to correlate them strictly with the physical changes in question, a task now being attempted by many American psychoanalysts. Coronary thrombosis, or rather the atheroma which makes this possible, and duodenal ulcer are among the conditions which have on good evidence been correlated with repressed anxiety. Even various skin diseases are thought to have a similar origin.

Psychoanalysis has been applied of late to the study of insanity more extensively than in previous years. Apart from the vexed question of the ultimate aetiology—whether this be toxic, hormonal or psychological—it is a matter of both theoretical and practical interest to ascertain not only why something has changed in the mind, but precisely what this change is. Detailed studies have been made of the structure and genesis of manic-depressive insanity, paranoia, and schizophrenia. Freud had elucidated the mechanisms of paranoia some years ago, but it is now known that the most characteristic of them—projection—is a constant accompaniment of infantile development. Indeed the tendency to project hostile or aggressive attitudes that are repressed in oneself on to the outer world is seldom altogether overcome even in adult life. The relationship between melancholia and normal grief has proved particularly interesting. In melancholia the object of hostility has become incorporated into the personality and the hatred of it, now expressed as hatred of the self, may, as is well known, be so intense as to lead to self-destruction. In mania, on the other hand, which so commonly alternates with melancholia, the self-hatred is for the time being not merely checked, but triumphantly overcome. In schizophrenia the dissociation which takes place in all nervous and mental disorders is much more pronounced than in any other, so the task of reuniting the dissociated elements is correspondingly greater, though at times not impossible.

The researches of the past twenty years have been

concerned much more with the aggressive impulses than with the sexual ones. This is not surprising, since Freud had so exhaustively investigated the latter in the early days of psychoanalysis that his work was popularly supposed to deal with nothing else. A number of analysts, however, formed the opinion that there had been in places some distortion in his conclusions arising from his viewing the problems in too one-sidedly masculine a fashion. In particular it has been thought that his conclusions on the sexual development of the female had been expressed too much as if the woman were *un homme manqué,* to the neglect of the earliest feminine attitude. It is true enough that most feminine infants pass through a stage in which they would masquerade as males, but I have pointed out that this is to a great extent a defense against a still earlier repressed femininity rather than, as Freud thought, a primary and normal stage of female development. This partial sex inversion is only one of a great number of defenses that the ego erects against the fundamental fear of sexuality, and Anna Freud has published a work in which she classifies and studies the various forms.

This all-pervading dread of sexuality, some of which may have leaked through into consciousness, is perhaps the most fateful agency in determining man's development. It has never been at all clear why it should be such a powerful thing, and the problem is evidently connected with the theological one of sin. Psychoanalysis is now, thanks very largely to the study of the unconscious in children, in a position to throw a great deal of light on the matter. Evidence is accumulating which goes to show that the real reason for the fear is the unfortunate circumstance that at their inception the sexual impulses are inextricably interwoven with aggressive ones, or else perhaps that they are intrinsically aggressive in their nature. The inevitable and constantly repeated thwartings stimulate these aggressive components and lead, as was mentioned earlier, to the most savage fantasies and impulses directed towards the most precious, loved and needed objects. Small wonder that the dread of destroying those loved ones is so terrifying to the infant's mind, and that he has to have recourse to all kinds of defensive measures which later come to constitute characteristics of his personality.

More extensive studies have been carried out on the non-sexual components of the primitive mind, more specially in connection with the aggressive impulses. These were briefly alluded to above when describing Melanie Klein's investigations in young children, and their importance cannot be exaggerated. Actually the essential nature itself of aggression is not known. It is not known if it arises from an independent instinct which becomes fused with the sexual ones. It is certainly here that it makes its most typical appearance, but it may be that the aggressiveness encountered is an inherent attribute of the sexual instinct and not a separate one. What is certain is that it is always intensified by any privation or thwarting of the sexual instinct, and it is this intensification that gives rise to so many of the deplorable aspects of humanity.

Freud himself regarded aggression as being originally an independent instinct, and he tried to connect it with a hypothetical "death instinct", i. e., an innate tendency of the organic to revert to the inorganic world. His view, however, has not been very widely accepted.

Mention was made earlier of the supposed influence our varying social institutions may have on the development of the unconscious mind. Far more important studies have been published in the last fifteen years on the reverse process to this: the influence the unconscious has on our social institutions and on the movements of political thought. This kind of work is a part of what is called Applied Psychoanalysis, i. e., the application of psychoanalytic knowledge to the study of various human activities.

An apparently remote contribution, but one of very great interest, is contained in Freud's last book *Moses and Monotheism.* In it he brought forward good reason for inferring that Moses was not a Jew but an Egyptian, and that the strict monotheism so characteristic of Judaism was directly derived from the teachings of the Egyptian King-heretic Akhenaten. He then traces much of Jewish psychology to the constant reaction against father murder, i. e., the oscillation between obedience to and the hatred for the primordial father. Freud also makes some valuable suggestions concerning the distressing, and socially important, problem of anti-Semitism. A number of other psychoanalysts have also tackled this difficult topic and have shown that its roots are far more complicated than is generally thought. It is, for instance, undoubtedly related to the "foreign body" fantasy of infants who have introjected their parents, with the consequent reaction against the introjected person. This topic is so overburdened with emotion and prejudice that the impartial elucidation of its roots will, it is hoped, in time be of practical value in coping with the painful problems involved.

The world events of the past thirty years have provided more than an ample supply of material for political economists and social psychologists to study. Since human motives, emotions, and impulses furnish the main driving force in all these affairs it is not surprising that psychoanalysts also have been able to make many contributions to our understanding of them, especially to the part played by the unconscious in influencing the various conscious attitudes. It is now becoming increasingly obvious that irrationality plays an unsuspectedly large part in political and social life, and this despite of the attempts to rationalize the attitudes irrational in origin. It is of course in respect of these irrational origins that psychoanalysis can make its most signal contributions.

The controversies in the field of economics during the 1930s revealed the extent to which deep-seated prejudices and subjective attitudes play a part in determining the various arguments, and a number of psychoanalysts, notably Money-Kyrle wrote books giving an exposition of the motives that often underlie apparently objective arguments.

The field of political and social psychology has

yielded even gloomier material for study than did the economic, though finally no sharp line can be drawn between them. The startling and disturbing war of "ideologies" revealed how extensively man's emotions had shifted from religious to mundane affairs, and this is surely to be correlated with the striking decay in religious belief during the past fifty or hundred years. We nowadays see attached to various political "movements" and "causes" the same spirit of devotion, self-sacrifice and idealism and the crusading spirit that was formerly almost a prerogative of religious beliefs, but unfortunately on the other hand also the same spirit of intolerance and persecution equally characteristic of religious movements.

Of the many shifting attitudes that go to make up these political and ideological movements I will here single out only two: the varying attitudes towards the ideas of freedom and of equality. With both of them there is, broadly speaking, a striking contrast between the nineteenth century and the twentieth. In the former a very high value was attached to the idea of freedom, and this found many forms of expression, poetical, political, economic, and so on. Passports were abolished, immigration freely permitted, and the freest interchange of trade, work, population, and domicile became a prevalent ideal. It was the age of nationalism which found its swan song in Wilson's plea for "self-determination". Social equality was little thought of; on the contrary, to rise in the social scale and improve one's lot seemed a laudable ambition. In our century we have witnessed an extensive reversal of all

these attitudes and this gives rise to interesting psychological problems.

The psychoanalyst finds a key to many of these
problems in the varying reciprocal strengths of the
ego and superego in different periods in the world's
history. The superego, it will be remembered, is developed in both sexes in close relationship to the idea
of the parent, perhaps particularly the father. It re-
tains this relationship throughout life and hence is
readily identified with or exchanged for prevailing
substitutes in the outer world, ruler, government, or
any superior. When the demands of the superego are
moderate, or when the ego feels more capable of coping with them, the person feels more confident in his
ability to look after himself without assistance from
the outside and is apt to rebel against what to him are
unnecessary restrictions. In other words, he is able to
turn against his superego and criticize its always excessive demands. Through the mechanism of projection this comes to mean an intolerance of restrictions
imposed by any authority. Previously subject nations
throw off what to them is the yoke of their oppressor,
and the activities even of one's own government are
often felt as impositions. Little or no guilt is felt at
having succeeded in life better than one's fellow,
though free play is left towards compassionate help for
the less fortunate. When on the contrary the claims of
the superego are present in a harsh and insistent
fashion, or when the ego is in comparison weak and
unable to cope with them, then the resulting social
picture is quite other. The ego can then find peace or

security only by yielding. At such a time we are told that what we need is a strong government, one which can save us and protect us from all our imagined dangers. The extreme of this is reached in the clamor for an all-powerful dictator to whom all responsibility for individual lives and personal decisions is given up, and who will issue instructions about every detail of conduct, opinions to be held, and daily activities. It is plain that these attitudes are not equally developed at the same time in all countries, and may even be very different in different continents; we have for example recently seen the contrast between the Indian cry for independence and self-rule and the startling docility exhibited by the German nation.

This is an exceedingly condensed outline of what in reality is a much more complex state of affairs in which many different tendencies interact in varying strengths and so produce a confused pattern. But, by and large, the outline appears to be valid, and so we reach the conclusion that the present generation is suffering from a much heavier burden of guilt—to be more accurate, of an unconscious sense of guiltiness—than did the preceding generation. It is not surprising, therefore, that the endeavors to escape from this intolerable burden are apt to assume desperate, panicky, and always irrational forms.

This sort of contrast can be presented in many different forms. To the one type, for instance, what his opponent sees as freedom appears as anarchy, while what he regards as a desirable state of order appears to the other to be intolerable restriction and oppression. What is certain is that no extreme attitude is ever pure. Even when it presents itself in the guise of a lofty idealism, and indeed contains genuine motives of that kind, this is only too apt to cover less laudable motives of avaricious greed and tyrannical mastery over one's fellows.

These last paragraphs are not quoted from other people's work. The contributions made by psychoanalysts, among which those of Professor Flugel are outstanding, to recent sociological problems are too extensive and numerous to be detailed here, but reference is made to the more important ones in the accompanying bibliography.

SELECTED BIBLIOGRAPHY

(In English)

The most valuable works are starred.

*Karl Abraham: *Selected Papers on Psycho-Analysis*. London, Hogarth Press, 1927.

Fr. Alexander: *The Medical Value of Psycho-analysis*. New York, W. W. Norton. Sec. Ed. 1936 (1932)

J. Bowlby: *Personality and Mental Illness*. London, Kegan Paul, 1940.

A. A. Brill: *Psychoanalysis*. Third Edition. Philadelphia, W. B. Saunders, 1922.

*A. A. Brill: *Fundamental Conceptions of Psycho-Analysis*. New York, Harcourt, Brace & Co., 1921.

A. A. Brill: *Freud's Contribution to Psychiatry*. New York, W. W. Norton, 1944.

A. A. Brill: *Lectures on Psychoanalytic Psychiatry*. New York, A. A. Knopf, 1946.

Helene Deutsch: *Psycho-Analysis of the Neuroses*. London, Hogarth Press, 1932.

Helene Deutsch: *Psychology of Women*. Two Vols. New York, Grune and Stratton, 1944-45.

*O. Fenichel: *The Psychoanalytic Theory of Neurosis*, New York, W. W. Norton, 1945.

*S. Ferenczi: *Contributions to Psycho-Analysis*, Boston, Richard S. Badger, 1916.

S. Ferenczi: *Further Contribution to the Theory and Technique of Psycho-Analysis*. London, Hogarth Press, 1926.

J. C. Flugel: *The Psycho-Analytic Study of the Family*. Sixth Ed. London, Hogarth Press, 1939.

123

Anna Freud: *The Ego and the Mechanisms of Defence.* New York, Int. Univ. Press, 1946.

*Sigm. Freud: *The Interpretation of Dreams.* Third Ed. London, Allen & Unwin, 1927.

*Sigm. Freud: *Three Contributions to Sexual Theory.* Fourth Ed. New York, Nervous and Mental Disease Publishing Co., 1930.

*Sigm. Freud: *Collected Papers.* Four Vols. London, Hogarth Press, 1924-25.

*Sigm. Freud: *Introductory Lectures on Psycho-Analysis.* London, Allen & Unwin, 1933.

*Sigm. Freud: *Inhibition, Symptom and Anxiety.* London, Hogarth Press, 1936.

Edward Glover: *Psycho-Analysis.* London, John Bale, 1939.

*Y. Hendrick: *Facts and Theories of Psychoanalysis.* New York, A. A. Knopf, 1939.

Ed. Hitschmann and Ed. Bergler: *Frigidity in Women.* New York, Nervous and Mental Disease Publishing Co., 1936.

Ernest Jones: *Treatment of the Neuroses.* London, Bailliere, Tindall & Cox, 1920.

Ernest Jones: *Papers on Psycho-Analysis.* Fourth Ed. Baltimore, Wm. Wood & Co., 1938.

*Melanie Klein: *Psycho-Analysis of Children.* London, Hogarth Press, 1937.

*Melanie Klein: *Contributions to Psycho-Analysis.* London, Hogarth Press.

*Melanie Klein and Joan Riviere: *Love, Hate and Reparation.* London, Hogarth Press, 1937.

M. Middlemore: *The Nursing Couple.* London, Hamish Hamilton, 1941.

R. Money-Kyrle: *The Development of the Sexual Impulses.* London, Kegan Paul, 1932.

J. J. Putnam: *Addresses on Psycho-Analysis.* London, Hogarth Press, 1921.

J. Rickman (Edited by) : *A General Selection from the Works of Freud.* London, Hogarth Press, 1937.

Ella Sharpe: *Dream Analysis*. London, Hogarth Press, 1937.
*G. Zilboorg and Henry, George W.: *A History of Medical Psychology*. New York, W. W. Norton, 1941.

APPLIED PSYCHO-ANALYSIS

Karl Abraham: *Dream and Myths*. Washington, Nervous and Mental Disease Publishing Co., 1913.

Fr. Alexander: *Our Age of Unreason*. Philadelphia, J. B. Lippincott, 1942.

E. Durbin and J. Bowlby: *Personal Aggressiveness and War*, London, Kegan Paul, 1939.

*J. C. Flugel: *Man, Morals and Society*. New York, Int. Univ. Press, 1946.

*Sigm. Freud:: *The Psychopathology of Everyday Life*. New York, MacMillan, 1930.

*Sigm. Freud: *Group Psychology and the Analysis of the Ego*. London, Hogarth Press, 1922.

*Sigm. Freud: *Totem and Taboo*. New York, New Republic Inc., 1931.

*Sigm. Freud: *Civilization, War and Death*. London, Hogarth Press, 1939.

Eric Fromm: *Escape from Freedom*. New York, Farrar & Rinehart, 1941.

*Edward Glover: *War, Sadism and Pacifism*. London, Allen & Unwin, 1933.

*S. Isaacs: *Social Development in Young Children*. London, Routledge, 1933.

Ernest Jones: *Essays in Applied Psycho-Analysis*. Second Ed. London, Hogarth Press, 1923.

Ernest Jones: *On the Nightmare*. London, Hogarth Press, 1931.

Ernest Jones (Edited by): *Social Aspects of Psycho-Analysis*. London, Williams & Norgate, 1924.

L. Kubie: *Practical Aspects of Psychoanalysis*. New York, W. W. Norton, 1936.

R. Laforgue: *Clinical Aspects of Psycho-Analysis*. London, Hogarth Press, 1938.

S. Lorand (Edited by): *Psychoanalysis Today*. New York, Int. Univ. Press, 1946.

S. Lorand: (Edited by): *Psychoanalysis Today*. New York, Int. Univ. Press, 1944.

Karl Menninger: *Man Against Himself*. New York, Harcourt, Brace & Co., 1938.

Karl Menninger: *Love Against Hate*. New York, Harcourt Brace & Co., 1942.

T. W. Mitchell: *The Psychology of Medicine*. London, Methuen & Co., 1921.

T. W. Mitchell: *Problems in Psychopathology*. London, Kegan Paul, 1927.

R. Money-Kyrle: *Aspasia*. London, Kegan Paul, 1932.

R. Money-Kyrle: *Superstition and Society*. London, Hogarth Press, 1939.

O. Rank: *The Myth of the Birth of the Hero*. Washington, Nervous and Mental Disease Publishing Co., 1914.

J. Rickman (Edited by): *On the Bringing up of Children*. London, Kegan Paul, 1936.

*G. Roheim: *The Origin and Function of Culture*. New York, Nervous and Mental Disease Publishing Co., 1943.

*Hanns Sachs: *The Creative Unconscious*. Boston, Sci-Art Publishers, 1942.

The *International Journal of Psycho-Analysis*, published by Bailliere, Tindall & Cox, is the official organ of the International Psycho-Analytical Association. *The International Psycho-Analytical Library* of books is published by the Institute of Psycho-Analysis and the Hogarth Press.